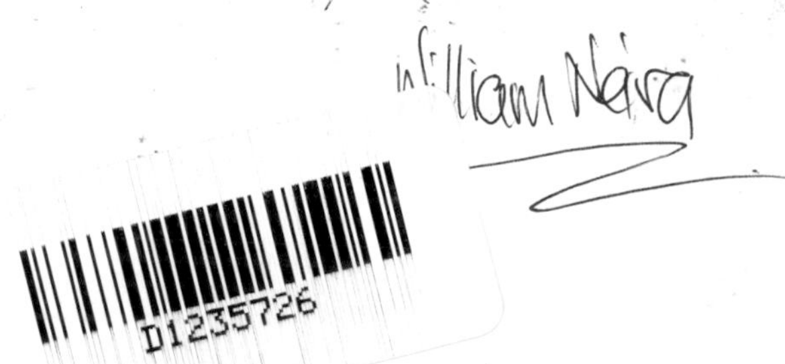

Romeo and Juliet

THE GRAPHIC NOVEL

William Shakespeare

Adapted from an original script by John McDonald

Australia • Brazil • Japan • Korea • Mexico • Singapore • Spain • United Kingdom • United States

Romeo and Juliet: The Graphic Novel
William Shakespeare

Publisher: Sherrise Roehr

Editor in Chief: Clive Bryant

Managing Development Editor: John Hicks

Associate Development Editor: Cécile Engeln

Director of U.S. Marketing: Jim McDonough

Director of Global Marketing: Ian Martin

Assistant Marketing Manager: Jide Iruka

Director of Production and Media Content: Michael Burggren

Associate Content Project Manager: Mark Rzeszutek

Print Buyer: Susan Spencer

Character Designs & Original Artwork: Will Volley

Lettering: Jim Campbell

Design and Layout: Jo Wheeler and Jenny Placentino

Compositor: MPS Limited, A Macmillan Company

Cover Designer: Gina Petti, Rotunda Design

Library of Congress Control Number: 2010925130

ISBN-13: 978-1-4240-4291-3

ISBN-10: 1-4240-4291-7

National Geographic Learning
20 Channel Center Street
Boston, MA 02210
USA

Cengage Learning is a leading provider of customized learning solutions with office locations around the globe, including Singapore, the United Kingdom, Australia, Mexico, Brazil, and Japan.

Cengage Learning products are represented in Canada by Nelson Education, Ltd.

Visit National Geographic Learning online at **ngl.cengage.com**

Visit our corporate website at **www.cengage.com**

Printed in China
7 8 9 16 15 14 13

Contents

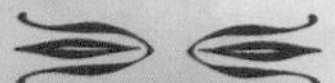

Romeo and Juliet

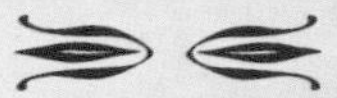

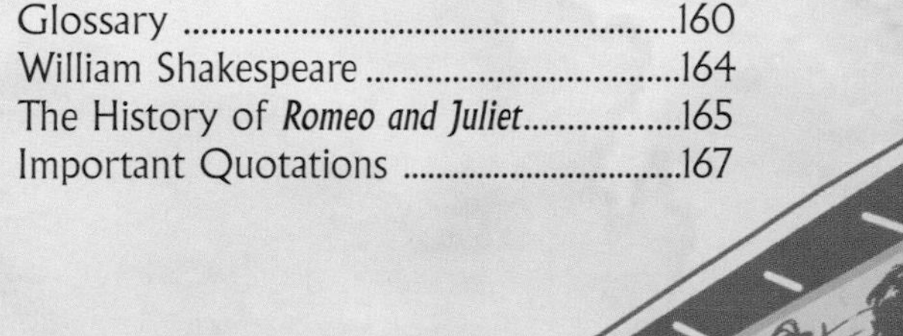

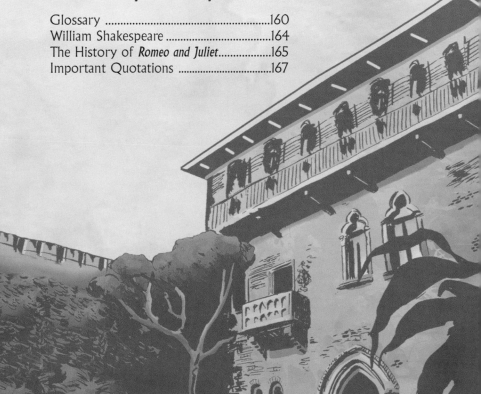

Characters

Romeo
Son of Lord Montague

Chorus
Introduces Acts I and II

Lord Montague
Head of the Montague family, which is feuding with the Capulet family

Lady Montague
Wife of Lord Montague

Benvolio
Lord Montague's ***nephew*** *and Romeo's friend*

Balthasar
A man who serves Romeo

Abraham
A man who serves Lord Montague

Prince Escalus
Prince of Verona

Mercutio
Relative of Prince Escalus and Romeo's friend

Count Paris
A young ***nobleman*** *who is related to Prince Escalus*

Juliet
Lord Capulet's daughter

Lord Capulet
Head of the Capulet family, which is feuding with the Montague family

Lady Capulet
Wife of Lord Capulet

Tybalt
Lady Capulet's ***nephew***

Nurse
Juliet's nurse

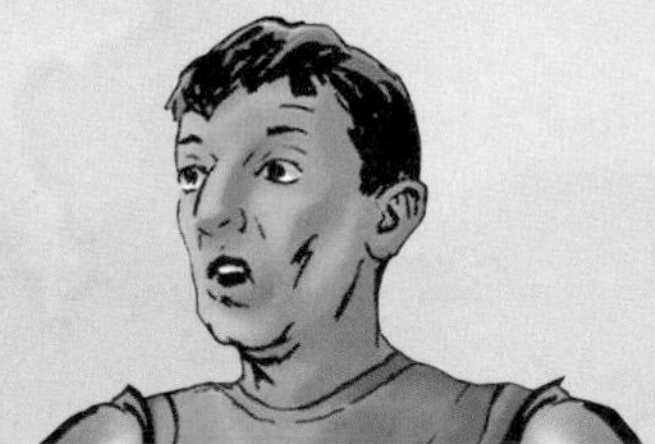

Peter
A man who serves Juliet's nurse

Sampson
A man who serves Lord Capulet

Gregory
A man who serves Lord Capulet

Friar Laurence
A monk

Friar John
A monk

Romeo and Juliet

Act I, Prologue
IN THE CITY OF VERONA, WHERE OUR STORY IS SET, LIVE TWO RICH AND POWERFUL FAMILIES, THE MONTAGUES AND THE CAPULETS. AN OLD **FEUD** RESTARTS BETWEEN THEM AND CLAIMS MANY BODIES.
ROMEO MONTAGUE AND JULIET CAPULET, SUPPOSED **ENEMIES,** FALL IN LOVE AT FIRST SIGHT.
ALTHOUGH THEIR LOVE ENDS IN **TRAGEDY,** THEIR DEATHS BRING PEACE AND END THE FIGHT.

THIS IS THE STORY OF THAT SAD ROMANCE –
– WHICH WE WILL NOW TELL.

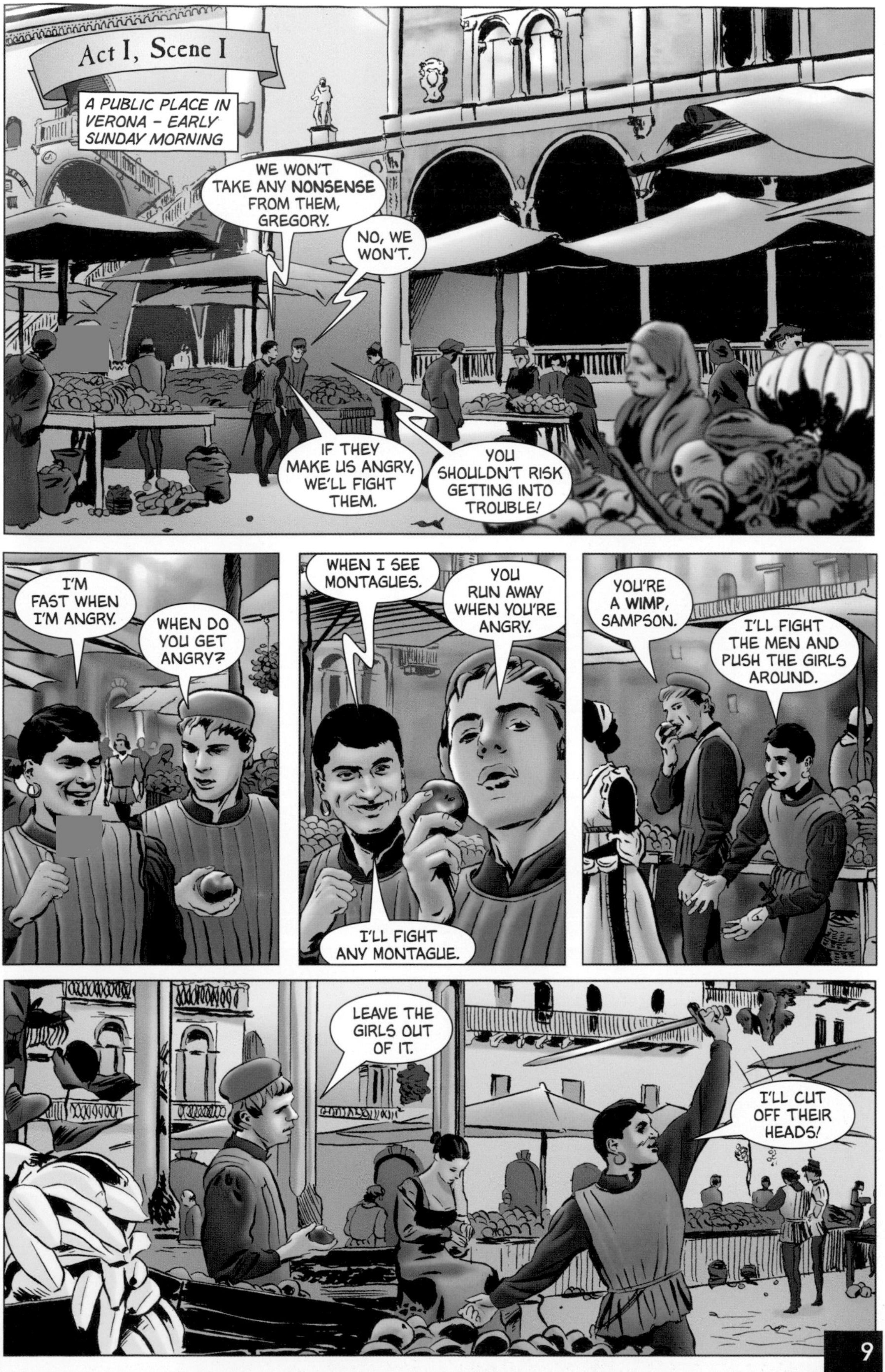

Act I, Scene I

A PUBLIC PLACE IN VERONA – EARLY SUNDAY MORNING

WE WON'T TAKE ANY **NONSENSE** FROM THEM, GREGORY.

NO, WE WON'T.

IF THEY MAKE US ANGRY, WE'LL FIGHT THEM.

YOU SHOULDN'T RISK GETTING INTO TROUBLE!

I'LL SHOW THEM WHO'S IN CHARGE.
YOU WILL?

OH, YES, I WILL!
HERE'S YOUR CHANCE. A COUPLE OF MONTAGUE'S MEN ARE COMING RIGHT NOW.

I'LL BACK YOU UP.
BY RUNNING AWAY?
DON'T WORRY ABOUT ME.
BUT I DO WORRY ABOUT YOU!

LET THEM START THE FIGHT.
I'LL GIVE THEM A DIRTY LOOK.
I'LL INSULT THEM BY BITING MY THUMB AT THEM.

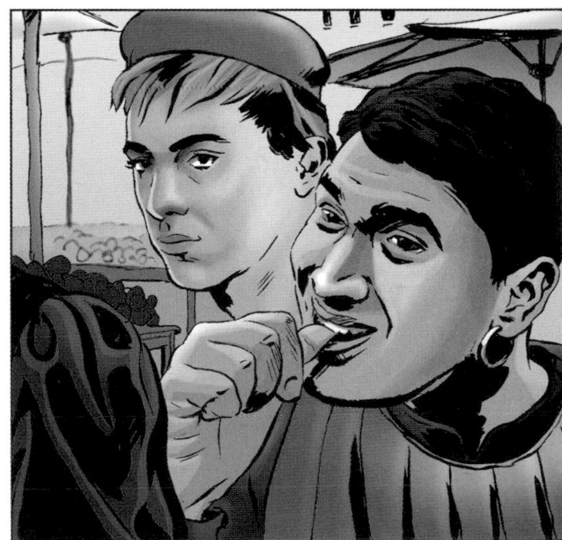

ARE YOU BITING YOUR THUMB AT US, SIR?
I AM BITING MY THUMB.

ARE YOU BITING YOUR THUMB AT US, SIR?
COULD I GET INTO TROUBLE IF I SAY "YES"?
YES.

THEN I AM NOT BITING MY THUMB AT YOU, BUT I AM BITING MY THUMB.
DO YOU WANT TO START A FIGHT?

NO, SIR.

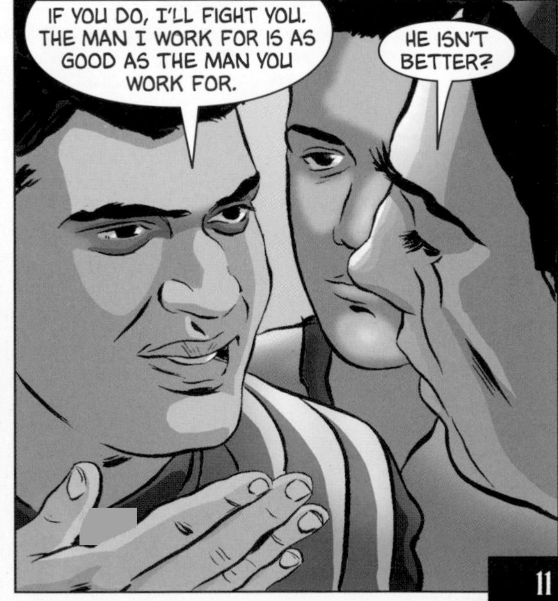
IF YOU DO, I'LL FIGHT YOU. THE MAN I WORK FOR IS AS GOOD AS THE MAN YOU WORK FOR.
HE ISN'T BETTER?

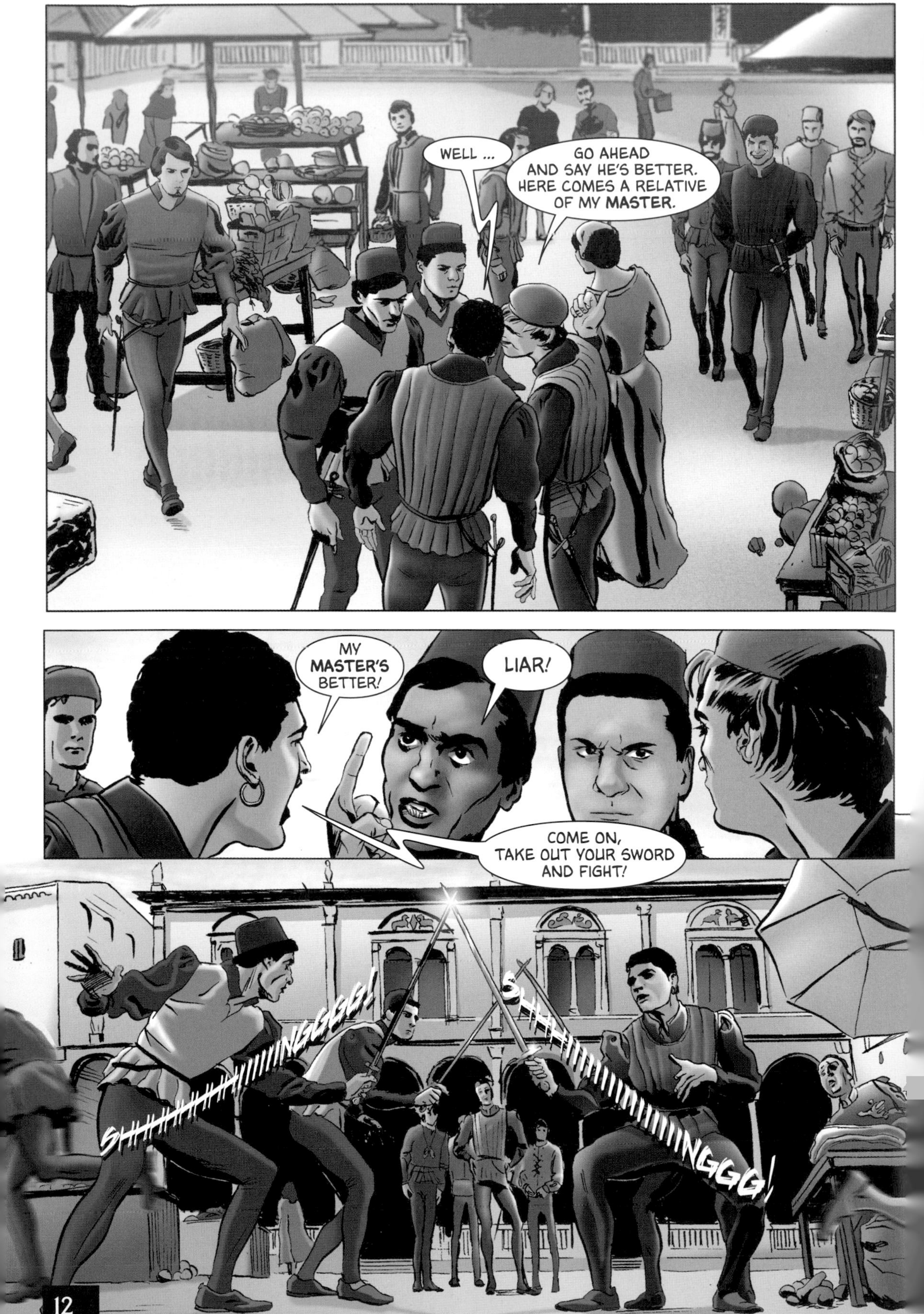

WELL ...
GO AHEAD AND SAY HE'S BETTER. HERE COMES A RELATIVE OF MY **MASTER**.

MY **MASTER'S** BETTER!
LIAR!
COME ON, TAKE OUT YOUR SWORD AND FIGHT!

SHHHHHHHIIIIIIINGGGG!
SHHHHIIIIIIIIIIIINGGG!

CLANG
KTANGG
OOF!
THUMP
STOP, YOU FOOLS!

CLANG
CLANG
AAAWK!

SWISH

SWOOOOOOOOOOSH

AAAH!
CRASH

CRASH
THWAK
SQUEEE
SQUEEE

IT'S THE CAPULETS AND MONTAGUES AGAIN!
WHACK
DOWN WITH THE CAPULETS!
DOWN WITH THE MONTAGUES!
THUD
THWAK
GIVE ME MY SWORD!
YOU NEED A **CRUTCH**, NOT A SWORD.
THERE'S OLD LORD MONTAGUE!
LORD CAPULET, YOU **VILLAIN**!
DON'T HOLD ME BACK!
YOU AREN'T GOING ANYWHERE!

TA-TAN TA RA!

WHAT'S THE MATTER WITH ALL OF YOU?

YOU'RE BEHAVING LIKE WILD ANIMALS!
STOP FIGHTING IMMEDIATELY!

THIS IS THE THIRD TIME THIS HAS HAPPENED – BECAUSE OF YOU, LORD CAPULET, AND YOU, LORD MONTAGUE!
THE PEOPLE OF VERONA HAVE HAD ENOUGH OF THIS.
IF IT HAPPENS AGAIN, I'LL HAVE THE PEOPLE WHO ARE RESPONSIBLE **EXECUTED.**

I WANT EVERYONE TO LEAVE.
COME WITH ME, LORD CAPULET.

I'LL DEAL WITH YOU THIS AFTERNOON, LORD MONTAGUE.

NOW, GO AWAY, ALL OF YOU!

WHO STARTED THIS, **NEPHEW**?
THE **SERVANTS**. I TRIED TO STOP THEM, BUT TYBALT CAME ALONG, LOOKING FOR TROUBLE.

HE PULLED HIS SWORD ON ME. AS WE WERE FIGHTING, MORE PEOPLE GOT INVOLVED. THEN THE PRINCE ARRIVED.

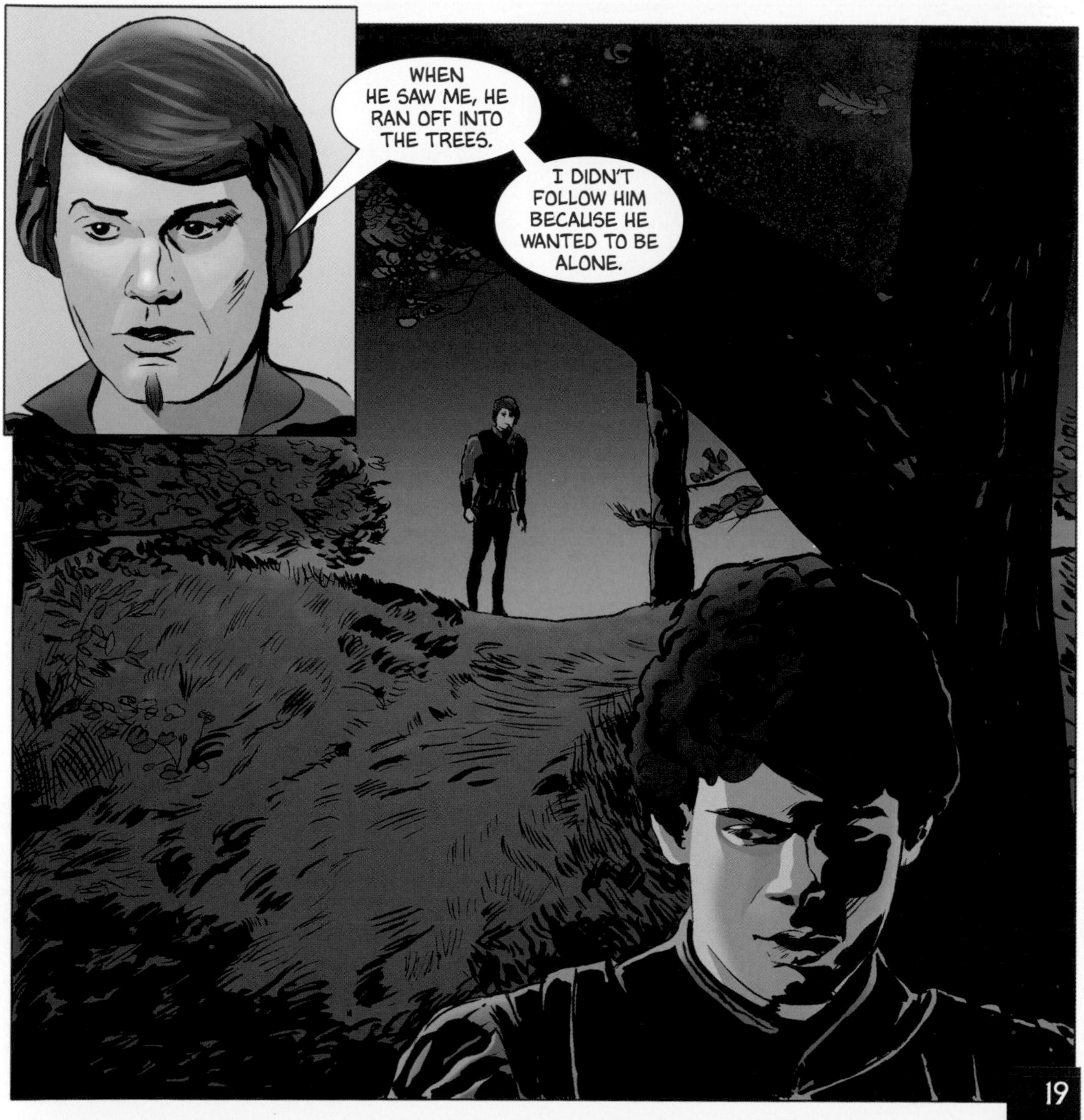

WHEN HE SAW ME, HE RAN OFF INTO THE TREES.

I DIDN'T FOLLOW HIM BECAUSE HE WANTED TO BE ALONE.

HE'S BEEN SEEN CRYING THERE MANY TIMES.
HE COMES BACK HOME WHEN THE SUN RISES. THEN, HE LOCKS HIMSELF IN HIS ROOM.

I WISH I KNEW WHAT WAS BOTHERING HIM.
HE WON'T TELL YOU, UNCLE?
NO.

HAVE YOU TRIED TO TALK WITH HIM?
HE WON'T TALK TO ANYONE.

HE IS KEEPING IT ALL INSIDE. IT ISN'T GOOD FOR HIM.

WE WOULD DO ANYTHING TO HELP HIM.
THERE HE IS!
LEAVE THIS TO ME – I'LL FIND OUT WHAT'S WRONG WITH HIM.

I HOPE HE TELLS YOU!

GOOD MORNING, COUSIN.

IT'S STILL MORNING?

IT'S NINE O'CLOCK.
TIME MOVES SLOWLY WHEN YOU'RE SAD.

WHY ARE YOU SO UNHAPPY?
BECAUSE I DON'T HAVE THE THING THAT WOULD MAKE ME HAPPY.
ARE YOU IN LOVE?

I AM!
THEN WHAT IS THE PROBLEM?
I'M IN LOVE WITH SOMEONE, BUT SHE ISN'T IN LOVE WITH ME.
LOVE CAN BE **CRUEL** SOMETIMES.

I THOUGHT LOVE WAS SUPPOSED TO BE BLIND, NOT CRUEL.

WHAT HAPPENED HERE?
DON'T TELL ME – THIS IS WHAT BOTH LOVE AND HATE CAN DO.

I WISH LOVE WOULD LEAVE ME ALONE!
LOVE IS HATE, AND HATE IS LOVE! LOVE IS EVERYTHING, AND IT IS NOTHING!
IT PRETENDS TO BE ONE THING, WHILE IT'S REALLY SOMETHING ELSE.

I AM IN LOVE, BUT LOVE HATES ME!

WHY AREN'T YOU LAUGHING?
SEEING YOU LIKE THIS MAKES ME SAD.

I APPRECIATE YOUR CONCERN, BUT YOUR SADNESS ISN'T HELPING ME.
IT WOULD BE BETTER IF YOU WOULD JUST LEAVE ME ALONE.

LOVE IS A PUZZLE, AND I JUST CAN'T UNDERSTAND IT.

GOOD-BYE, COUSIN.
LET ME COME WITH YOU.

COME WITH ME?
I'M NOT EVEN HERE MYSELF!

WHO ARE YOU IN LOVE WITH?
I DON'T WANT TO TALK ABOUT IT.
JUST TELL ME!

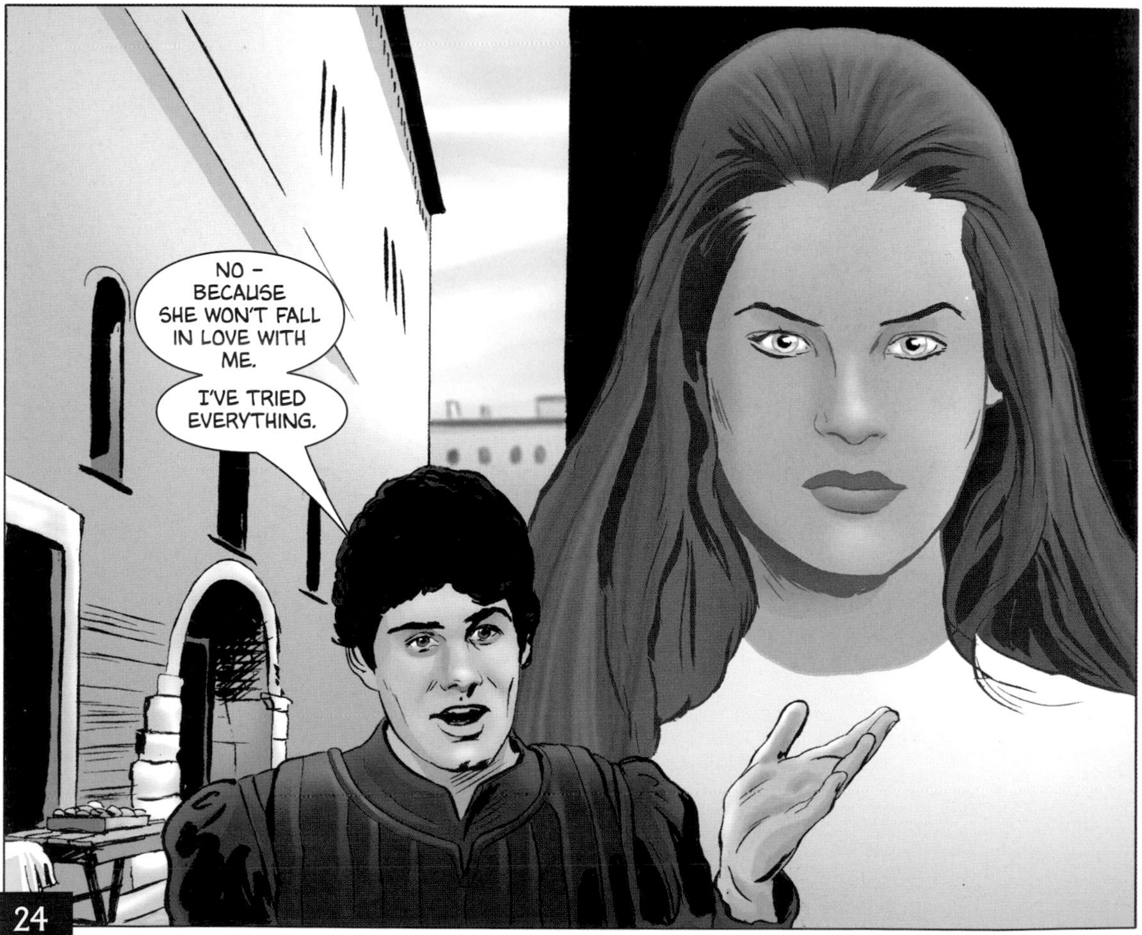

NO – BECAUSE SHE WON'T FALL IN LOVE WITH ME.

I'VE TRIED EVERYTHING.

FORGET ABOUT HER!

HOW?

THERE ARE PLENTY OF OTHER GIRLS.

NOT LIKE HER.

I JUST CAN'T FORGET ABOUT HER. ANY OTHER GIRL WOULD ONLY REMIND ME OF HER.

GOOD-BYE! YOU CAN'T MAKE ME FORGET HER.
I'LL FIND A WAY.

Act I, Scene II
A STREET IN VERONA – SUNDAY MORNING
LORD MONTAGUE AND I HAVE TO STOP OUR FAMILIES FROM FIGHTING.
IT'S TOO BAD THAT YOU HAVE BEEN **ENEMIES** FOR SO LONG.
NOW, WHAT IS YOUR ANSWER TO MY REQUEST?

MY DAUGHTER IS STILL VERY YOUNG. SHE ISN'T EVEN FOURTEEN YET.
MAYBE IN A YEAR OR TWO.
GIRLS EVEN YOUNGER THAN THAT GET MARRIED.

EARLY MARRIAGE CAN BE BAD FOR A GIRL. WHY DON'T YOU GET TO KNOW HER BETTER?
IF SHE AGREES TO MARRIAGE, THEN I WON'T STAND IN YOUR WAY.

I'M HAVING A PARTY HERE TONIGHT.
WHY DON'T YOU COME? THERE WILL BE MANY LOVELY GIRLS TO DANCE WITH.

WHEN YOU SEE ALL THE BEAUTIFUL YOUNG LADIES OF VERONA HERE TONIGHT, YOU MIGHT CHANGE YOUR MIND ABOUT MY DAUGHTER.

MY **SERVANT**,
GO AND INVITE THE PEOPLE ON THIS LIST TO MY PARTY TONIGHT.

HOW CAN I INVITE THE PEOPLE ON THIS LIST? I CAN'T READ!
I'LL HAVE TO FIND SOMEONE WHO CAN.

FIND SOMEONE ELSE. YOU'LL FORGET ALL ABOUT HER SOON!

I'M GOING TO KICK YOU IN A MINUTE!
WHY WOULD YOU DO THAT?
ARE YOU CRAZY?

I MIGHT AS WELL BE.

GOOD AFTERNOON.
CAN YOU READ, SIR?
ONLY MY OWN **FORTUNE.**
CAN YOU READ THIS WRITING?

YES, IF I KNOW WHAT IT SAYS.
AH, THEN, GOOD DAY, SIR.

WAIT! I CAN READ.

COUNT ANSELME, PLACENTIO, MERCUTIO, VALENTINE, TYBALT, ROSALINE –
THESE ARE INVITATIONS.
WHERE'S THE PARTY?

AT OUR HOUSE.
WHOSE HOUSE?
MY **MASTER'S.**

WHO IS YOUR **MASTER?**
THE GREAT, RICH LORD CAPULET.
WHY DON'T YOU COME TO THE PARTY – AS LONG AS YOU'RE NOT A MONTAGUE!
GOOD-BYE!

SO ... ROSALINE'S GOING TO BE AT THIS PARTY.
WE HAVE TO GO. THEN YOU CAN COMPARE HER TO THE OTHER GIRLS.
AND I BET YOU WON'T THINK SHE'S SO BEAUTIFUL AFTER THAT!

THERE ISN'T A WOMAN ALIVE WHO IS MORE BEAUTIFUL THAN ROSALINE!

LET'S PROVE IT, THEN – AT LORD CAPULET'S PARTY.

ALL RIGHT, I'LL GO. BUT ONLY BECAUSE ROSALINE WILL BE THERE.

Act I, Scene III
THE CAPULETS' HOUSE - SUNDAY AFTERNOON
WHERE'S MY DAUGHTER, NURSE?

CALL HER FOR ME.

I ASKED HER TO BE HERE.

JULIET!

WHO WANTS ME?
YOUR MOTHER.

WHAT'S THE MATTER?

LEAVE US ALONE FOR A LITTLE WHILE, NURSE.

NO, WAIT - YOU SHOULD HEAR THIS, TOO.

YOU KNOW MY DAUGHTER IS AT A CERTAIN AGE.
I KNOW HER EXACT AGE.
SHE' ISN'T FOURTEEN YET.
HOW LONG IS IT UNTIL AUGUST?

JUST OVER TWO WEEKS.
SHE'LL BE FOURTEEN JUST BEFORE AUGUST - THE EXACT SAME AGE AS MY DEAR DEAD DAUGHTER, SUSAN.

IT'S BEEN ELEVEN YEARS SINCE THE EARTHQUAKE. I'LL NEVER FORGET IT. WE WERE SITTING OUTSIDE BY A WALL –

– EVERYTHING SHOOK, AND I RAN AWAY AS QUICKLY AS I COULD.
THAT WAS ELEVEN YEARS AGO.
SHE COULD STAND ON HER OWN THEN AND RUN AROUND.
ONE DAY SHE FELL OVER AND HURT HER HEAD. MY HUSBAND PICKED HER UP. HE SAID,
"YOU'LL FALL ON YOUR BACK WHEN YOU ARE SMARTER, WON'T YOU, JULIET?"

SHE STOPPED CRYING AND SAID, "YES."
I'LL NEVER FORGET IT!

ENOUGH! BE QUIET!
BANG

YES, MADAM, BUT I CAN'T HELP LAUGHING WHEN I THINK ABOUT IT.

"YOU'LL FALL ON YOUR BACK WHEN YOU ARE SMARTER," SAID MY HUSBAND.
SHE STOPPED CRYING AND SAID, "YES."
STOP, NURSE. PLEASE!

I'M FINISHED! YOU WERE SUCH A PRETTY BABY.
I DREAM OF SEEING YOU MARRIED SOME DAY.

THAT'S WHAT I WANTED TO TALK TO YOU ABOUT.
WOULD YOU LIKE TO GET MARRIED, JULIET?

IT'S AN HONOR THAT I HAVEN'T REALLY THOUGHT ABOUT.
AN HONOR! YOU COULDN'T HAVE GOTTEN SUCH WISDOM FROM ME!

WELL, THINK ABOUT IT NOW.
GIRLS YOUNGER THAN YOU GET MARRIED. I GAVE BIRTH TO YOU WHEN I WAS ABOUT YOUR AGE.
THE HONORABLE COUNT PARIS WANTS TO MARRY YOU.

OH, LADY! WHAT A WONDERFUL MAN!
THE BEST IN VERONA.

HE'LL BE AT THE PARTY TONIGHT.
YOU CAN SEE FOR YOURSELF JUST HOW WONDERFUL HE IS.

ALL HE NEEDS NOW TO MAKE HIMSELF COMPLETE IS A BEAUTIFUL WIFE.

THE TWO OF YOU WILL MAKE A PERFECT COUPLE.
YOU'LL SHARE EVERYTHING HE HAS. YOU WON'T LOSE A THING.
LOSE? NO – YOU'LL GET BIGGER. MEN MAKE WOMEN BIGGER.

CAN YOU LOVE HIM?
I'LL TRY TO LIKE HIM, MOTHER, IF THAT IS WHAT YOU WANT.

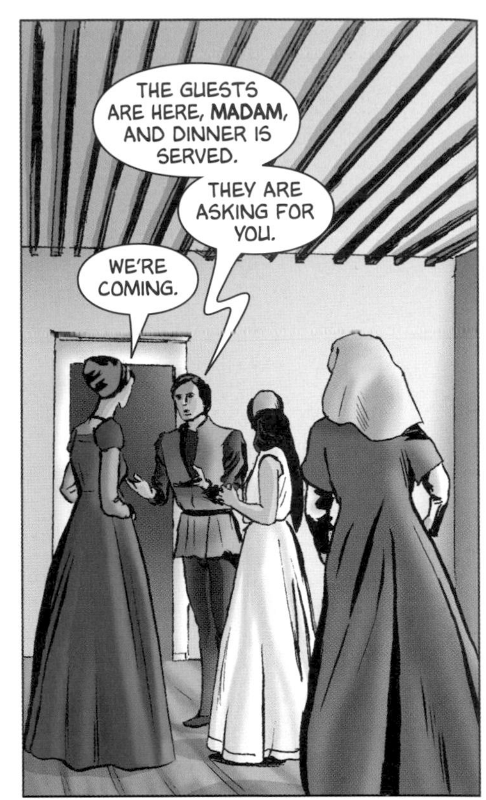
THE GUESTS ARE HERE, **MADAM**, AND DINNER IS SERVED.
THEY ARE ASKING FOR YOU.
WE'RE COMING.

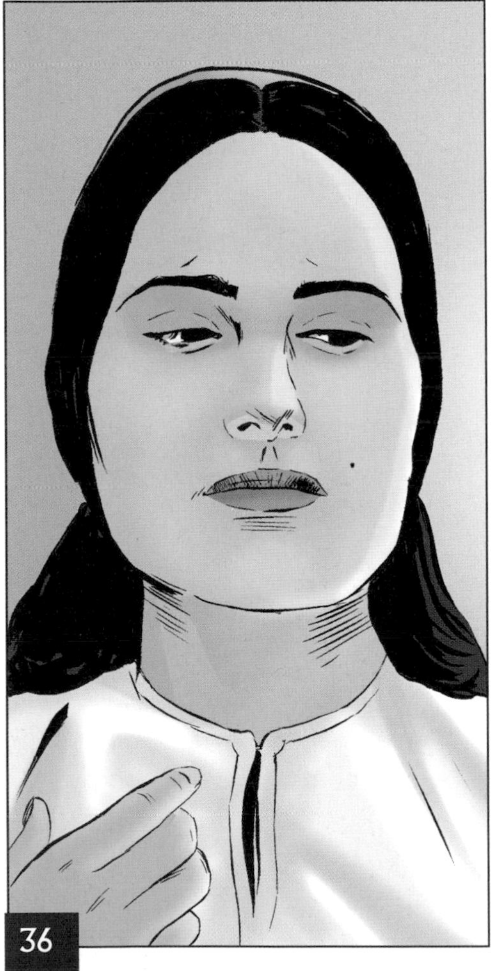

JULIET, COUNT PARIS IS WAITING.
GO ON, GIRL. YOUR FUTURE IS WAITING FOR YOU.

Act I, Scene IV

NEAR THE CAPULETS' HOUSE – SUNDAY EVENING

WHAT WILL WE SAY WHEN PEOPLE ASK US WHY WE'RE HERE?

WE DON'T NEED TO WORRY ABOUT THAT.

WE DON'T EVEN NEED TO INTRODUCE OURSELVES.
WE'LL JUST DANCE AND LEAVE.
I'M TOO SAD TO DANCE.

BUT YOU HAVE TO DANCE, ROMEO.
NO. YOU CAN DANCE IF YOU WANT TO.

YOU'RE A LOVER. YOU HAVE TO DANCE!
I CAN'T - LOVE HAS HURT ME.
YOU CAN'T BLAME LOVE. IT WILL ONLY MAKE YOU SADDER.
I DON'T CARE. LOVE HAS BEEN TOO CRUEL TO ME.
THEN BE CRUEL BACK! FORGET ABOUT LOVE!
GIVE ME A MASK TO COVER MY FACE.
AN UGLY MASK HIDES AN UGLY FACE!
COME ON - ONCE WE'RE IN, WE'LL ALL DANCE.
NOT ME. I WON'T DANCE!
DON'T BE SUCH A STICK-IN-THE-MUD! COME ON. LET'S GO!
WE'RE WASTING DAYLIGHT.
BUT IT'S NIGHT!

I MEAN FIRELIGHT – STOP BEING SO PICKY!
I KNOW WE DON'T MEAN TO DO ANY HARM, BUT I DON'T THINK GOING TO THE PARTY IS A GOOD IDEA.
WHY NOT?
I HAD A DREAM LAST NIGHT.
SO DID I.
WHAT WAS YOURS ABOUT?
THAT DREAMERS OFTEN LIE.
ONLY WHEN THEY'RE DREAMING.
YOU'VE BEEN VISITED BY QUEEN MAB, THE FAIRY WHO MAKES DREAMS,
ALONG WITH HER TEAM OF TINY CREATURES.
SHE RIDES IN A NUTSHELL, WITH SPIDERS' LEGS FOR SPOKES.
THE COVER IS A GRASSHOPPER WING. HER DRIVER IS A TINY FLEA.

SHE VISITS LOVERS' BRAINS EVERY NIGHT AND FILLS THEM WITH DREAMS OF LOVE.
SHE DRIVES THROUGH PEOPLE'S MINDS AND MAKES THEM WANT ALL SORTS OF THINGS.
SHE MAKES THEM GREEDY, DANGEROUS, BRAVE, AND FRIGHTENED.

THEY WAKE UP, SAY A PRAYER, AND FALL ASLEEP AGAIN.
QUEEN MAB TWISTS THE NIGHT AND TURNS IT INTO A **NIGHTMARE.**
SHE **RUINS** YOUNG GIRLS.
SHE –
STOP, MERCUTIO!
YOU'RE TALKING **NONSENSE.**
YOU'RE RIGHT.
DREAMS ARE **NONSENSE** BECAUSE THEY CHANGE FASTER THAN THE WIND.
COME ON, WE'RE GOING TO BE LATE!
I HAVE A BAD FEELING ABOUT THIS.
SOMETHING'S GOING TO HAPPEN HERE TONIGHT – SOMETHING THAT MAY BRING MY SAD LIFE TO AN EARLY END.
IT'S ALL IN GOD'S HANDS NOW.
LET'S GO!
BEAT THE DRUM!
B-DUM B-DUM

Act I, Scene V
INSIDE THE CAPULETS' HOUSE – SUNDAY EVENING
WHERE'S POTPAN?
WE SHOULDN'T HAVE TO DO ALL THE WORK!

CLEAR AWAY THE STOOLS AND THE PLATES.
ANTONY! POTPAN!

YES, I'M READY.
THEY'RE CALLING FOR YOU.
I CAN'T BE THERE AND HERE AT THE SAME TIME
COME ON, BOYS!

WELCOME, GENTLEMEN!
THE LADIES THAT DON'T HAVE CORNS ON THEIR FEET WILL DANCE WITH YOU.

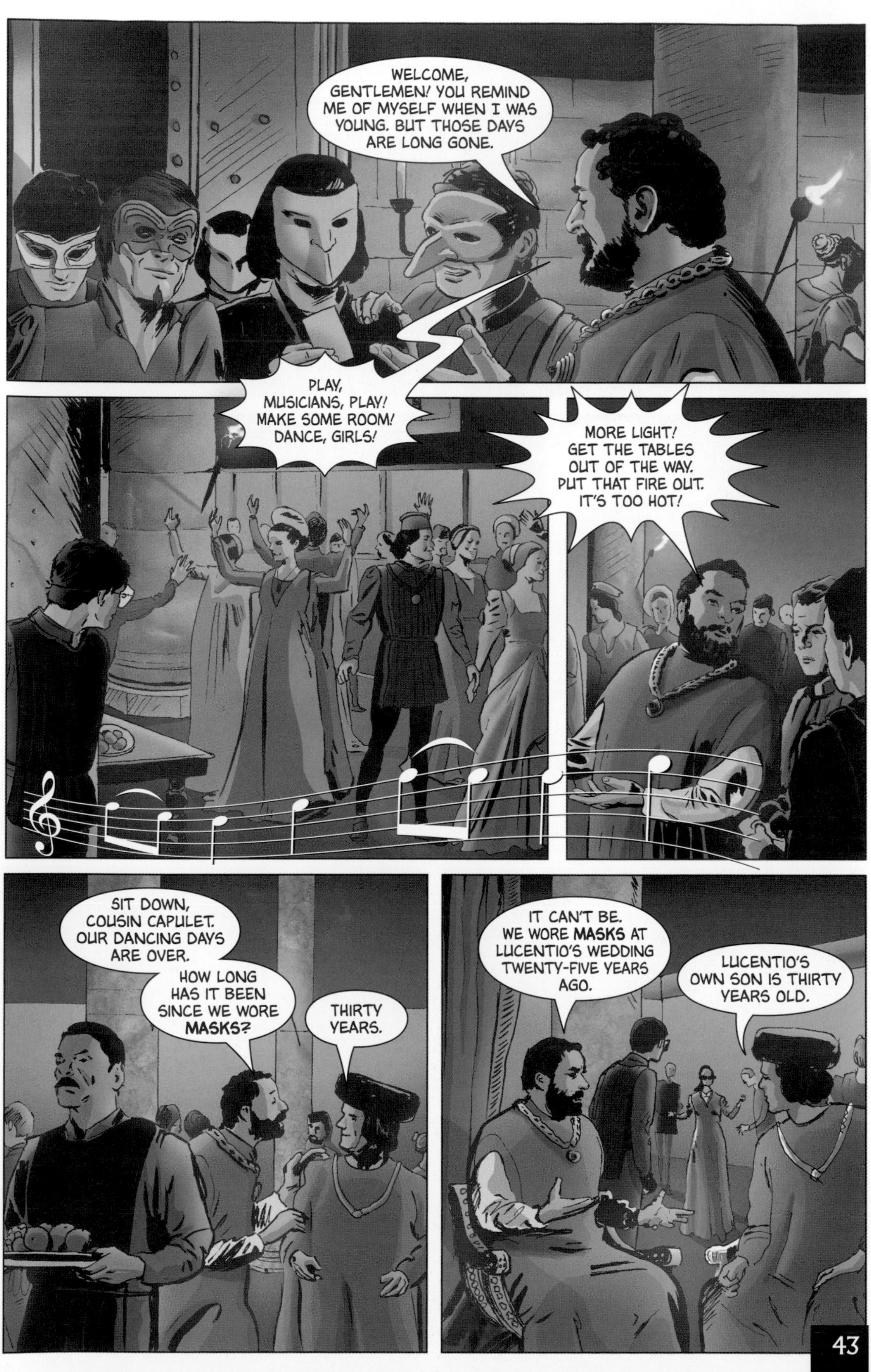

WELCOME, GENTLEMEN! YOU REMIND ME OF MYSELF WHEN I WAS YOUNG. BUT THOSE DAYS ARE LONG GONE.

PLAY, MUSICIANS, PLAY! MAKE SOME ROOM! DANCE, GIRLS!

MORE LIGHT! GET THE TABLES OUT OF THE WAY. PUT THAT FIRE OUT. IT'S TOO HOT!

BUT HIS SON WAS JUST A CHILD TWO YEARS AGO!

WHO'S THAT GIRL DANCING WITH THAT **NOBLEMAN** OVER THERE?
I DON'T KNOW, SIR.

SHE'S SO BEAUTIFUL!

I'LL TALK TO HER AFTER THIS DANCE. HOW COULD I HAVE THOUGHT THAT I WAS IN LOVE BEFORE?
I've never seen real beauty until now.

THAT MAN IS A MONTAGUE!
GET MY SWORD, BOY.

TYBALT! WHERE ARE YOU GOING?
UNCLE, THERE IS A MONTAGUE –
OUR **ENEMY**!

IT'S YOUNG ROMEO, ISN'T IT?
YES – THAT **VILLAIN** ROMEO.
CALM DOWN. LEAVE HIM ALONE.
HE ISN'T CAUSING ANY TROUBLE.

I DON'T WANT ANY TROUBLE AT THIS PARTY.
JUST **IGNORE** HIM.
THAT'S AN ORDER!

BUT HE'S OUR **ENEMY**! I WON'T PUT UP WITH IT.
YOU WILL PUT UP WITH IT!
I'M IN CHARGE HERE, AND I DON'T WANT ANYONE TO UPSET MY GUESTS.

BUT, UNCLE –
ENOUGH!

ENJOY, EVERYBODY!

ACCEPT IT OR LEAVE THE PARTY.

MORE LIGHT!

DO WHAT I SAY.

ENJOY!

ALL RIGHT, I'LL GO. BUT THE MONTAGUES ARE GOING TO BE SORRY!

MY HAND IS NOT GOOD ENOUGH TO TOUCH SOMETHING SO PERFECT. I HOPE MY HAND DOESN'T UPSET YOU.
IF IT DOES, LET ME MAKE UP FOR IT WITH A KISS FROM MY LIPS.

IT DOESN'T UPSET ME. IT SHOWS GOOD MANNERS. **HOLY** PEOPLE **EMBRACE** BY TOUCHING **PALMS**.

DON'T **HOLY** PEOPLE HAVE LIPS, TOO?

YES. THEY USE THEM TO PRAY WITH.
THEN CAN WE JOIN OUR LIPS AND ANSWER MY PRAYER?

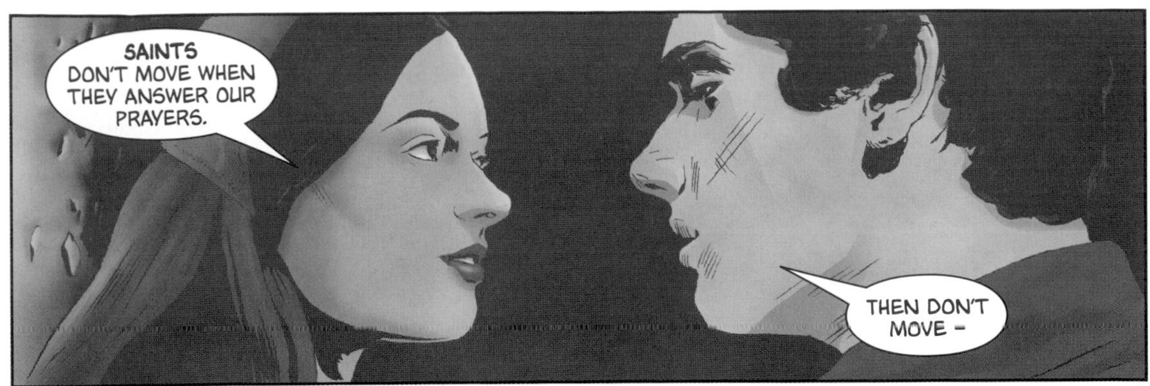
SAINTS DON'T MOVE WHEN THEY ANSWER OUR PRAYERS.
THEN DON'T MOVE –

THERE. ALL MY SIN IS GONE.
NOW MY LIPS HAVE YOUR SIN.
LET ME TAKE IT BACK.

YOUR KISS IS SO **FORMAL**.

MADAM, YOUR MOTHER WANTS TO TALK TO YOU.

WHO IS HER MOTHER?
HER MOTHER IS THE LADY OF THIS HOUSE.
I NURSED HER DAUGHTER, THE GIRL YOU WERE JUST TALKING TO.
WHOEVER MARRIES HER HAS TO COME FROM A GOOD FAMILY.

SHE'S A CAPULET! MY LIFE IS IN MY **ENEMY'S** HANDS!
LET'S LEAVE.
YES, WE SHOULD LEAVE.

THANK YOU FOR COMING, GENTLEMEN.
I NEED MORE LIGHT HERE!

IT'S GETTING LATE. LET'S GO TO BED.

NURSE ...

WHO IS THAT?
TIBERIO'S SON.

AND THAT MAN, THERE?
YOUNG PETRUCHIO.
AND THE PERSON FOLLOWING HIM?

I DON'T KNOW.

GO AND ASK HIS NAME. PLEASE TELL ME HE ISN'T ALREADY MARRIED.
HIS NAME IS ROMEO, AND HE'S A MONTAGUE.

How can the man I love be the son of people I hate?
It's so unfair!

WHAT'S WRONG?
NOTHING.

JULIET!
JUST A MINUTE!

LET'S GO. ALL THE GUESTS ARE GONE.

Act II, Prologue
ROMEO'S LOVE FOR ROSALINE DIED, EVEN THOUGH FOR HER HE CRIED.
AND EVEN THOUGH SHE'S A CAPULET, ROMEO NOW LOVES JULIET.
AND JULIET FEELS THE SAME, EVEN WITH THE PROBLEMS CAUSED BY THEIR LAST NAMES.
TRUE LOVE WAS BORN TONIGHT. BUT THEY HAVE TO KEEP THAT LOVE OUT OF SIGHT.
ALTHOUGH THEY CANNOT MEET DURING THE DAY,
TRUE LOVE ALWAYS FINDS A WAY.

Act II, Scene I
OUTSIDE THE CAPULETS' ORCHARD – AFTER MIDNIGHT, MONDAY MORNING
ROMEO!
I CAN'T LEAVE WITHOUT SEEING HER.
HE WENT HOME.
HE RAN THIS WAY AND JUMPED OVER THE ORCHARD WALL.
ROMEO! ARE YOU THERE?
SAY SOMETHING!
...
HE CAN'T HEAR ME, AND I CAN'T HEAR HIM.
ROMEO! DID YOU FORGET ABOUT ROSALINE?

YOU'LL MAKE HIM ANGRY.
NO, I WON'T. BUT HE'D BE ANGRY IF HE THOUGHT SOMEONE ELSE WAS WITH ROSALINE.
I'M JUST USING ROSALINE'S NAME TO GET HIM TO RESPOND.
HE'S HIDING IN THE **ORCHARD**. LEAVE HIM ALONE!
THEN SIT THERE AND DREAM OF ROSALINE!
SMASH
GOOD NIGHT, ROMEO!
LET'S GO.
Act II, Scene II
THE ORCHARD AT THE CAPULETS' HOUSE - AFTER MIDNIGHT, MONDAY MORNING
THEY CAN MAKE ALL THE JOKES THEY WANT.

BUT, WAIT! WHAT IS THAT LIGHT SHINING THROUGH THAT WINDOW?
IT IS THE EAST, AND JULIET IS THE SUN!
RISE, BEAUTIFUL SUN, AND MAKE THE **JEALOUS** MOON DISAPPEAR.
IT IS **JEALOUS** OF YOUR BEAUTY.
SHE IS MY LOVE!
SHE SEEMS TO BE SPEAKING, BUT NOT TO ME.
HER EYES ARE LIKE STARS!
SHE LOOKS SO BEAUTIFUL, LEANING HER CHEEK ON HER HAND.
I WISH I WAS A GLOVE ON THAT HAND, SO THAT I COULD TOUCH HER CHEEK.

OH, MY!
SHE'S SPEAKING.
SPEAK AGAIN, MY ANGEL!
OH, ROMEO, ROMEO!
WHY DO YOU HAVE TO BE A MONTAGUE?
FORGET YOUR FATHER AND CHANGE YOUR NAME. OR I'LL CHANGE MINE.
MAYBE I SHOULD SAY SOMETHING.
IT'S ONLY YOUR NAME THAT IS MY **ENEMY**.
BUT WHAT IS "MONTAGUE"?
IT DOESN'T MEAN ANYTHING.
NAMES AREN'T IMPORTANT.
THE FLOWER THAT WE CALL A ROSE WOULD SMELL JUST AS SWEET EVEN IF IT WAS CALLED SOMETHING ELSE.
ROMEO WOULD BE JUST AS PERFECT IF HE WAS CALLED SOMETHING ELSE.
GIVE UP YOUR NAME, ROMEO. YOU CAN HAVE ME IN **EXCHANGE** FOR IT.
JUST SAY YOU LOVE ME,
AND I'LL NEVER BE ROMEO AGAIN.
WHO'S HIDING DOWN THERE?

I DON'T WANT TO SAY MY NAME BECAUSE YOU HATE IT.
I KNOW WHO YOU ARE. YOU'RE ROMEO MONTAGUE.
NOT IF YOU HATE THAT NAME.
HOW DID YOU GET HERE? AND WHY DID YOU COME?
THE WALLS ARE SO HIGH. MY FAMILY WILL KILL YOU IF THEY FIND YOU HERE.
I FLEW OVER THE WALL ON THE WINGS OF LOVE.
YOUR FAMILY CAN'T STOP ME.
IF THEY SEE YOU, THEY'LL MURDER YOU.
IF YOU LOVE ME, THEN THEY CAN'T HURT ME.
I DON'T WANT THEM TO FIND YOU HERE.
IF YOU DON'T LOVE ME, LET THEM FIND ME.
I'D RATHER DIE THAN LIVE WITHOUT YOUR LOVE.
WHO TOLD YOU HOW TO GET HERE?

LOVE TOLD ME. I WOULD HAVE FOUND YOU ANYWHERE, NO MATTER WHERE YOU WERE.
I'M EMBARRASSED BECAUSE OF WHAT YOU HEARD ME SAY TONIGHT.
I WANT TO TAKE THE WORDS BACK, BUT I CAN'T.
DO YOU LOVE ME?
YOU'LL SAY "YES" EVEN IF IT'S A LIE.
TELL ME THE TRUTH.
DO YOU REALLY LOVE ME? BECAUSE I LOVE YOU, ROMEO MONTAGUE.
BUT IF YOU THINK I'M TOO EASY TO CATCH, I'LL **PLAY HARD TO GET**.
IT'S TOO LATE FOR THAT NOW! I HAVE **REVEALED** MY HEART TO YOU. MY LOVE FOR YOU IS REAL.
I CAN'T TAKE BACK WHAT I SAID. PLEASE TAKE MY LOVE SERIOUSLY.
DEAR LADY, I **SWEAR** – ON THE MOON ABOVE.
GASP!
OH, DON'T **SWEAR** ON THE MOON. IT CHANGES EVERY MONTH.
I DON'T WANT YOUR LOVE TO CHANGE THE WAY THE MOON DOES.
WHAT SHOULD I **SWEAR** BY?

DON'T **SWEAR** AT ALL. OR IF YOU HAVE TO **SWEAR**, **SWEAR** ON YOURSELF SINCE YOU ARE THE GOD I **WORSHIP**. THEN, I'LL BELIEVE YOU.
IF THE LOVE IN MY HEART –
NO! DON'T **SWEAR**. IT'S TOO SOON TO MAKE PROMISES. THIS IS ALL HAPPENING TOO FAST.
GOOD NIGHT, MY LOVE!
IF THIS LOVE IS REAL, IT WILL GROW STRONGER WITH TIME.
GOOD NIGHT! SLEEP WELL!
DON'T LEAVE ME THIS WAY.
WHAT DO YOU MEAN?
I NEED A PROMISE OF YOUR LOVE.
I GAVE YOU THAT BEFORE YOU ASKED FOR IT. BUT I WISH I COULD TAKE IT BACK.
WHY?
SO I COULD GIVE IT TO YOU AGAIN.
MY LOVE FOR YOU IS ENDLESS.

JULIET?
I HEAR A NOISE. GOOD-BYE!
JULIET!
COMING, NURSE!
STAY HERE. I'LL COME BACK.
THIS HAS TO BE A DREAM. IT'S TOO GOOD TO BE TRUE!
I HAVE TO GO, ROMEO.
IF YOU TRULY LOVE ME, I'LL SEND SOMEONE TO YOU TOMORROW. TELL THAT PERSON A TIME AND PLACE FOR OUR MARRIAGE, AND WE'LL BE TOGETHER FOREVER.
MADAM!
COMING!
BUT IF YOU DON'T MEAN IT, THEN –
MADAM!
I'M COMING!
– THEN STAY AWAY FROM ME. I'LL SEND SOMEONE TOMORROW.
MY LIFE DEPENDS ON IT.
GOOD NIGHT, A THOUSAND TIMES!

I'M A THOUSAND TIMES WORSE OFF WITHOUT YOU.
LOVE LEAVES LOVE SLOWLY, WITH A HEAVY HEART.
PSST! ROMEO!
I WISH I COULD CALL HIM BACK. IF I DIDN'T HAVE TO BE QUIET –
– I WOULD SHOUT OUT HIS NAME UNTIL MY THROAT WAS SORE!
ROMEO!
IS THAT MY **SOUL**, WHISPERING MY NAME?
HOW SOFT AND SWEET IT SOUNDS.
ROMEO!
MY LOVE?
WHAT TIME SHOULD I SEND THE MESSENGER TO YOU?
NINE O'CLOCK.
TOMORROW FEELS LIKE IT'S TWENTY YEARS AWAY.
I FORGOT WHY I CALLED YOU BACK.
I'LL STAND HERE UNTIL YOU REMEMBER.
I WISH YOU COULD STAY HERE FOREVER.
I WILL IF YOU WANT ME TO.

IT'S ALMOST MORNING.
YOU HAVE TO GO. BUT I'D LIKE TO PULL YOU BACK LIKE A BIRD ON A STRING.
I WISH YOU COULD.
SO DO I.
GOOD NIGHT AGAIN. LEAVING EACH OTHER IS SWEET BUT FILLED WITH **SORROW**. I WILL SAY GOOD NIGHT TO YOU UNTIL IT IS TOMORROW!
SLEEP PEACEFULLY. I'LL GO SEE FRIAR LAURENCE RIGHT AWAY.

Act II, Scene III

FRIAR *LAURENCE'S CHURCH, NEAR VERONA – EARLY MONDAY MORNING*

THE SUN IS GOING TO RISE SOON.

I HAVE TO FILL THIS BASKET WITH HERBS AND **HEALING** PLANTS BEFORE THE SUN COMES UP.
THE EARTH GIVES US BOTH LIFE AND DEATH. AND, WHEN THINGS DIE, THEY RETURN TO THE EARTH.

EVERY HERB AND PLANT IS DIFFERENT. SOME CAN **HEAL**, AND SOME CAN DO **HARM**. BUT ALL OF THEM HAVE A PURPOSE.

THERE'S NOTHING ON EARTH THAT DOESN'T HAVE SOME GOOD IN IT. BUT EVERYTHING CAN ALSO BE USED THE WRONG WAY.

THERE'S BOTH **POISON** AND MEDICINE INSIDE THIS SMALL FLOWER.
IT SMELLS SWEET, BUT YOU WOULD DIE IF YOU ATE IT.
THIS MIX OF GOOD AND **EVIL** IS IN PEOPLE, TOO.
GOOD MORNING, **FRIAR** LAURENCE.

ROMEO! YOU DON'T USUALLY WAKE UP THIS EARLY.

SOMETHING HAS TO BE WRONG, YOU HAVEN'T GONE TO SLEEP AT ALL, HAVE YOU?
YOU'RE RIGHT. I HAVEN'T.

GOD FORGIVE YOU!
WERE YOU WITH ROSALINE?
NO, **FRIAR**. I'VE FORGOTTEN ALL ABOUT HER!
THAT'S GOOD.

BUT WHERE HAVE YOU BEEN?
AT A PARTY WITH MY **ENEMY**. AT THE PARTY, I WAS HURT BY SOMEONE WHO WAS ALSO HURT BY ME. ONLY YOU CAN **HEAL** US.
IT WILL HELP MY **ENEMY** AS MUCH AS IT WILL HELP ME.

I DON'T UNDERSTAND.

I'M IN LOVE WITH LORD CAPULET'S DAUGHTER!
WE'RE IN LOVE WITH EACH OTHER, AND WE NEED TO GET MARRIED AS SOON AS POSSIBLE.

I'LL TELL YOU ALL ABOUT IT LATER.
PLEASE, MARRY US TODAY!
OH, MY GOODNESS! HOW DID YOU FORGET ROSALINE SO QUICKLY?

YOUNG MEN LOVE WITH THEIR EYES, NOT WITH THEIR HEARTS.
HOW MANY TEARS DID YOU CRY FOR ROSALINE?

I CAN STILL HEAR YOUR SIGHS AND GROANS.
I CAN SEE THE STAINS FROM YOUR TEARS ON YOUR CHEEKS.
DID YOU REALLY FEEL STRONGLY ABOUT ROSALINE?

HOW CAN YOUR FEELINGS HAVE CHANGED SO QUICKLY?
YOU USED TO SCOLD ME FOR LOVING ROSALINE.

FOR BEING **OBSESSED** WITH HER, YES.
YOU TOLD ME TO **BURY** MY LOVE.
YES, NOT TO **EXCHANGE** IT FOR ANOTHER!

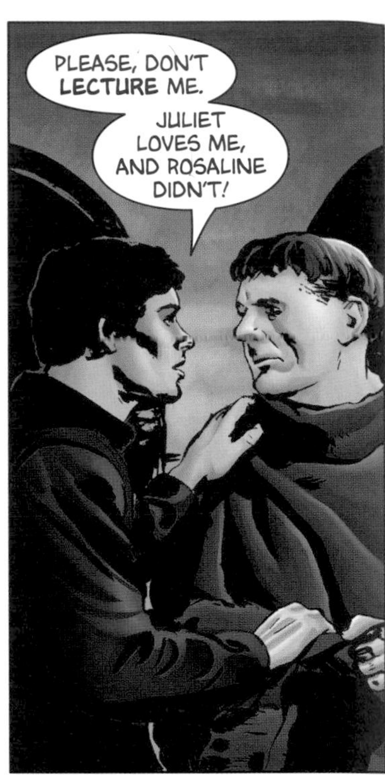
PLEASE, DON'T **LECTURE** ME.
JULIET LOVES ME, AND ROSALINE DIDN'T!

THAT'S BECAUSE SHE KNEW YOU DIDN'T REALLY LOVE HER!

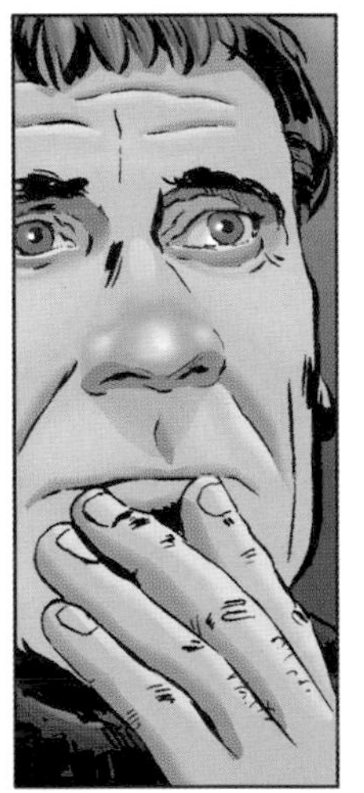

I WILL HELP YOU FOR ONE REASON. THIS MIGHT CREATE PEACE BETWEEN YOUR TWO FAMILIES.
THEN LET'S MOVE QUICKLY!

CRASH

WISELY AND SLOWLY. PEOPLE WHO RUN USUALLY FALL DOWN.

Act II, Scene IV
A STREET IN VERONA – MONDAY MORNING
WHERE'S ROMEO? DID HE COME HOME LAST NIGHT?
NOT TO HIS FATHER'S HOUSE.

THAT ROSALINE IS DRIVING HIM CRAZY!
TYBALT SENT A LETTER TO THE MONTAGUE HOUSE.
BANG

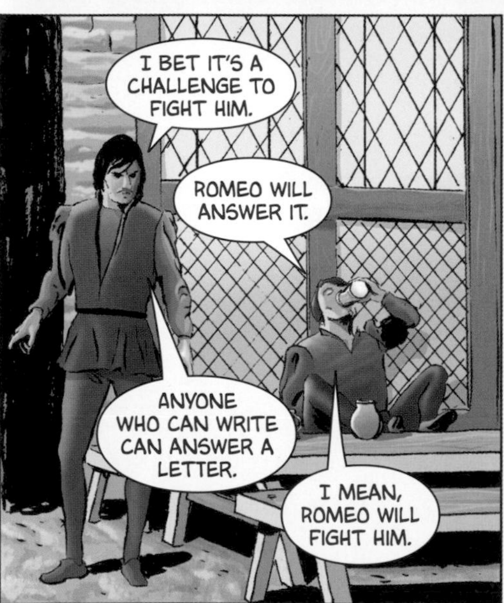
I BET IT'S A CHALLENGE TO FIGHT HIM.
ROMEO WILL ANSWER IT.
ANYONE WHO CAN WRITE CAN ANSWER A LETTER.
I MEAN, ROMEO WILL FIGHT HIM.

ROMEO'S ALREADY DEAD. HE'S BEEN KILLED BY HIS LOVE FOR ROSALINE.
HE CAN'T FIGHT TYBALT.
WHAT'S SO GREAT ABOUT TYBALT?

HE'S AN EXCELLENT SWORD FIGHTER! HE KNOWS ALL THE MOVES – EVEN THE HAI!
THUD
THE WHAT?

THE MOVE THAT KILLS! I HATE **SHOW OFFS** WITH BIG MOUTHS LIKE HIM!

HERE COMES ROMEO!

LIKE A **LIMP** FISH.
THE ONLY THING HE'LL TALK ABOUT IS HOW LOVELY ROSALINE IS.
ROMEO, YOU DESERTED US LAST NIGHT.

GOOD MORNING!

SORRY, MERCUTIO. I HAD SOME BUSINESS TO TAKE CARE OF.
YES, FUNNY BUSINESS!

THE BUSINESS WAS SO IMPORTANT THAT I COULDN'T WORRY ABOUT COURTESY.
OH, REALLY?
I AM THE DEFINITION OF **COURTESY**.

BUT TELL ME THIS - WHO WERE YOU **CURTSEYING** TO?

I'LL SHOW YOU THE SOLE OF MY SHOE, BUT I WILL NOT SHARE WHAT IS IN MY **SOUL** WITH YOU.
VERY FUNNY. WHEN YOUR SHOE IS WORN OUT, THAT JOKE WILL STILL BE PRETTY **LAME**.

I TELL MY JOKES SOLELY TO ENTERTAIN YOU.
STOP HIM, BENVOLIO! I'M LOOSING THIS CONTEST OF WITS!

COME ON!
I CAN'T COMPETE WITH YOU.

YOUR JOKES ARE BITING - LIKE A SPICY SAUCE.

A SAUCE LIKE THAT WOULD BE A GOOD THING TO SERVE ON A SILLY GOOSE LIKE YOU.
OH, NO. THAT'S TOO MUCH!

YOU'RE NO FUN.
ISN'T THIS BETTER?
YOU'RE ACTING LIKE YOURSELF AGAIN INSTEAD OF WALKING AROUND LIKE SOME LOVESICK IDIOT.

ENOUGH.
DO YOU WANT ME TO STOP TALKING?

YOU TALK TOO MUCH.
BUT I WAS ALMOST FINISHED.
LOOK! THIS SHOULD BE FUN!

HERE COMES A LARGE SHIP!
THERE ARE TWO OF THEM!

PETER!
YES, MA'AM?

GIVE ME MY FAN, PETER.
YES, PETER. GIVE HER THE FAN TO HIDE HER FACE.

GOOD MORNING, GENTLEMEN.
GOOD AFTERNOON, DEAR LADY.
IS IT AFTERNOON?
IT IS. WOULD YOU LIKE TO COME BACK HOME WITH ME AND CHECK THE TIME?

GET AWAY FROM ME! WHAT KIND OF MAN ARE YOU?
WHACK

GENTLEMEN, CAN YOU TELL ME WHERE I CAN FIND YOUNG ROMEO?
I CAN TELL YOU. I'M ROMEO.

GOOD.
IS IT GOOD?
IF YOU'RE ROMEO, I'D LIKE TO SPEAK WITH YOU PRIVATELY.

PRIVATELY?
YOU KNOW WHAT I SEE?
WHAT?

AN OLD STALE MARE.
AN OLD MARE, ISN'T GOOD ANYWHERE. IT SMELLS, AND IT'S TOUGH, AND IT'S FAR TOO ROUGH!
SWISH

ROMEO, ARE YOU COMING WITH US TO YOUR FATHER'S HOUSE FOR DINNER?
I'LL BE THERE SOON.

GOOD-BYE,
OLD LADY.

LADY, LADY,
LADY ...
GOOD-BYE!

WHO WAS
THAT RUDE
MAN?
SOMEONE
WHO LOVES THE
SOUND OF HIS
OWN VOICE.

I'D TAKE HIM
DOWN A PEG
OR TWO!
I'M NOT
ONE OF HIS LOOSE
WOMEN OR SOMEONE
WHO HOLDS HIS
KNIVES.

YOU STOOD
THERE AND LET
HIM INSULT
ME!
WHACK
HE DIDN'T
INSULT YOU. I'D HAVE
THREATENED HIM IF HE
HAD INSULTED
YOU.
I'M JUST
AS BRAVE AS ANY
MAN!

I'M SHAKING
WITH ANGER!
THE DIRTY
VILLAIN!

SIR, AS I
SAID, JULIET
ASKED ME TO
FIND YOU.
NOW, I HOPE
YOU'RE NOT TRYING TO
TAKE ADVANTAGE OF HER.
SHE'S VERY YOUNG, AND IT
WOULD BE TERRIBLE FOR
YOU TO PLAY SUCH A
DIRTY TRICK.

NURSE,
I HAVE TO
PROTEST –
YOU'RE
A GOOD MAN, AND
I'LL TELL HER THAT.
SHE'LL BE VERY
HAPPY.
TELL HER
WHAT?

THAT YOU "**PROTEST.**" THAT'S WHAT A GENTLEMAN WOULD DO.
JUST TELL HER TO GO TO FRIAR LAURENCE'S CHURCH THIS AFTERNOON.

TAKE THIS FOR YOUR TROUBLE.

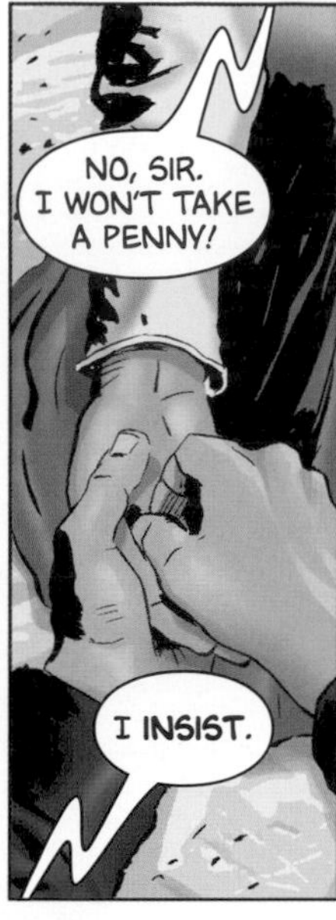
NO, SIR. I WON'T TAKE A PENNY!
I INSIST.

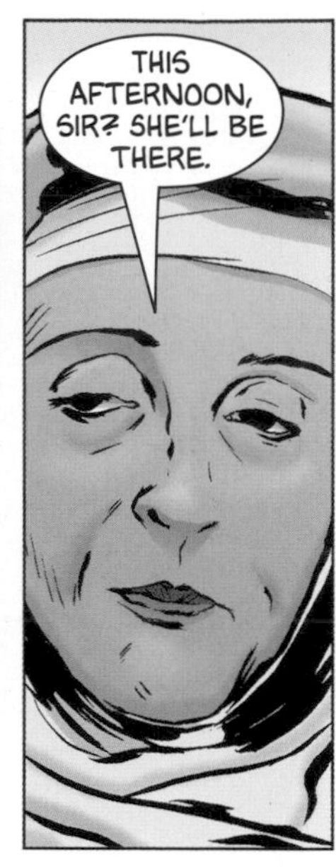
THIS AFTERNOON, SIR? SHE'LL BE THERE.

IF YOU WAIT BEHIND THE **ABBEY** WALL, MY **SERVANT** WILL BRING YOU A LADDER MADE OF ROPE.
I'LL USE THAT TONIGHT TO CLIMB UP TO THE ROOM OF MY DREAMS.

GOOD-BYE! TELL JULIET I SEND MY LOVE.
LISTEN, SIR –

WHAT IS IT?
CAN YOUR **SERVANT** BE TRUSTED?

YES, HE CAN.

WELL, THERE'S A **NOBLEMAN** CALLED COUNT PARIS WHO WANTS TO MARRY JULIET. BUT SHE DOESN'T WANT TO MARRY HIM.

"ROSEMARY" AND "ROMEO" BOTH BEGIN WITH THE SAME LETTER, RIGHT?
YES, THEY BOTH BEGIN WITH THE LETTER "R."
DON'T MAKE FUN OF ME! THAT'S THE NOISE A DOG MAKES.
JULIET SAYS THE NICEST THINGS ABOUT YOU – AND ROSEMARY.

GIVE HER MY LOVE!
I WILL.

PETER!
YES?

WALK IN FRONT OF ME. QUICKLY!
WHACK

Act II, Scene V
THE CAPULETS' GARDEN – MONDAY AFTERNOON
NURSE SAID SHE'D BE BACK IN HALF AN HOUR.
WHAT'S TAKING HER SO LONG?

IT'S BEEN THREE HOURS SINCE SHE LEFT.

OLD PEOPLE ARE SO SLOW.

IF SHE WAS YOUNGER, SHE'D MOVE FASTER.
OH, HERE SHE COMES!

DID YOU SEE HIM, NURSE?
WAIT HERE, PETER.

WHAT'S THE MATTER?
WHY IS YOUR FACE SO SAD?
TELL ME THE NEWS, WHETHER IT'S GOOD OR BAD.
I'M TIRED. GIVE ME A MINUTE. MY BONES ACHE FROM ALL THAT RUNNING!

HURRY, NURSE. PLEASE TELL ME!
WAIT A MINUTE! CAN'T YOU SEE THAT I'M OUT OF BREATH?

JUST ANSWER THIS QUESTION – IS THE NEWS GOOD OR BAD?
JUST SAY "GOOD" OR "BAD," AND I'LL WAIT FOR THE REST OF THE STORY.

I THINK YOU'VE MADE A BAD CHOICE. ROMEO MIGHT BE GOOD-LOOKING, BUT HE'S NOT VERY POLITE.
BUT DO WHATEVER YOU WANT. HAVE YOU HAD LUNCH YET?

WHAT DID HE SAY ABOUT OUR MARRIAGE?
FLING...

I HAVE A TERRIBLE HEADACHE! AND MY BACK HURTS.
YOU SHOULD BE **ASHAMED** FOR SENDING ME ALL THE WAY OUT THERE.

I'M SORRY YOU DON'T FEEL WELL, BUT PLEASE TELL ME WHAT ROMEO SAID!

ROMEO ACTED LIKE AN **HONORABLE** GENTLEMAN.
WHERE'S YOUR MOTHER?

SHE'S INSIDE! WHAT KIND OF ANSWER IS THAT?
"ROMEO ACTED LIKE AN **HONORABLE** GENTLEMAN. WHERE'S YOUR MOTHER?"
YOU'RE SO IMPATIENT!

IF THIS IS HOW YOU THANK ME, YOU CAN DO YOUR OWN DIRTY WORK FROM NOW ON.
MY GOODNESS!
WHAT DID ROMEO SAY?
CAN YOU GET TO FRIAR LAURENCE'S CHURCH TODAY?

I CAN.

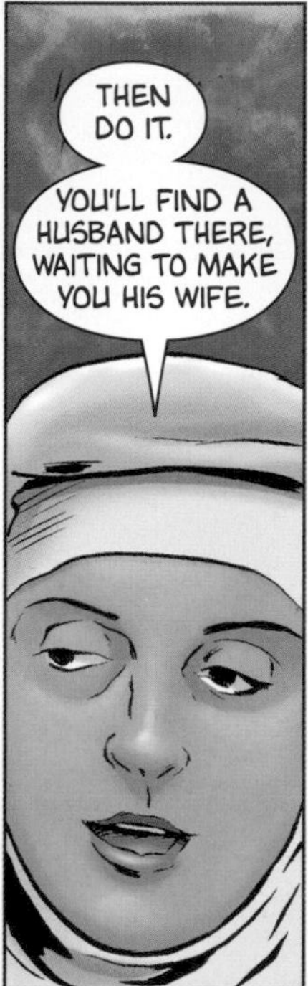
THEN DO IT.
YOU'LL FIND A HUSBAND THERE, WAITING TO MAKE YOU HIS WIFE.

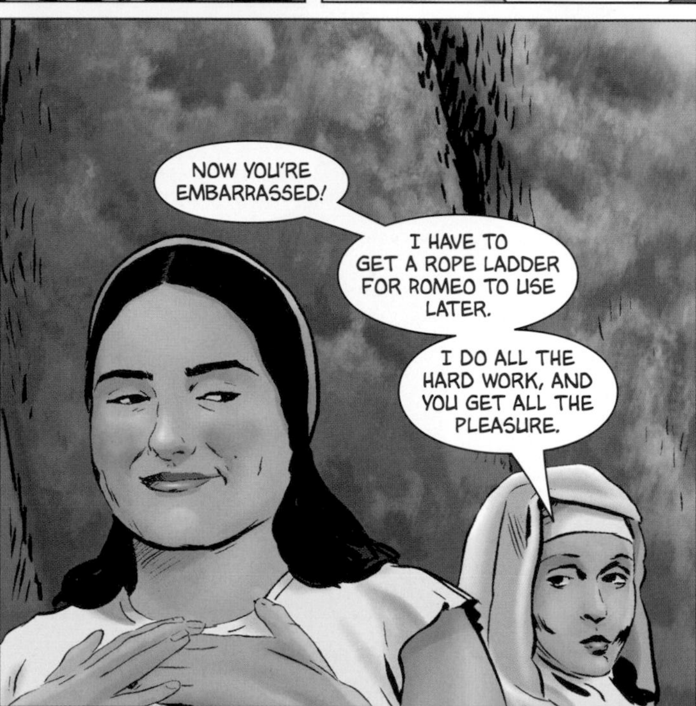
NOW YOU'RE EMBARRASSED!
I HAVE TO GET A ROPE LADDER FOR ROMEO TO USE LATER.
I DO ALL THE HARD WORK, AND YOU GET ALL THE PLEASURE.

I'M GOING TO LUNCH.
HURRY TO THE CHURCH.
I WILL. GOOD-BYE, DEAR NURSE.

Act II, Scene VI
FRIAR LAURENCE'S CHURCH – MONDAY AFTERNOON
MAY HEAVEN BLESS THIS HOLY MARRIAGE. I HOPE YOU DON'T LIVE TO REGRET THIS.
WE WON'T. NOTHING BAD CAN HAPPEN. EVEN IF I DIED RIGHT AFTER MARRYING JULIET, I WOULD DIE A HAPPY MAN.

SUCH PASSION CAN LEAD TO A PASSIONATE END. GOING TOO FAST IS JUST AS BAD AS GOING TOO SLOWLY.

HERE COMES JULIET.
SHE LOOKS SO LOVELY!

GOOD EVENING, FRIAR LAURENCE.
ROMEO IS READY, DEAR GIRL.
AND SO AM I.

JULIET, IF YOU'RE AS HAPPY AS I AM NOW, IMAGINE HOW HAPPY WE WILL BE AFTER WE GET MARRIED!
WORDS AREN'T ENOUGH TO DESCRIBE IT. MY LOVE IS SO GREAT! IT CANNOT BE MEASURED.

LET US BEGIN.

Act III, Scene I

A PUBLIC PLACE IN VERONA – LATER, MONDAY AFTERNOON
LET'S GO, MERCUTIO. THERE'S TROUBLE IN THE AIR. IF WE MEET ANY CAPULETS, WE'LL MOST LIKELY END UP FIGHTING WITH THEM. THIS HOT WEATHER MAKES PEOPLE ANGRY.

YOU'RE A TROUBLEMAKER, BENVOLIO.
AM I?

YOU **LOSE YOUR TEMPER** FASTER THAN ANYONE ELSE IN ITALY.
FOR WHAT REASON?
FOR ANY REASON.

YOU'D FIGHT WITH A MAN BECAUSE OF THE LENGTH OF HIS BEARD, OR THE COLOR OF HIS EYES – ANYTHING!

ALL YOUR FIGHTING HAS MADE YOU CRAZY.
CLUCK CLUCK
ONE TIME, YOU FOUGHT WITH A MAN BECAUSE HE COUGHED AND WOKE UP YOUR DOG.
ANOTHER TIME, YOU FOUGHT WITH A MAN BECAUSE YOU DIDN'T LIKE HIS CLOTHES!

AND ANOTHER TIME, YOU FOUGHT WITH A MAN WHO USED OLD LACES TO TIE HIS NEW SHOES.
SO DON'T TELL ME TO CONTROL MYSELF!
IF I FOUGHT AS MUCH AS YOU DO, I WOULDN'T LIVE VERY LONG.
SQUAARK!

HERE COME THE CAPULETS.
I DON'T CARE!

FOLLOW ME. I'LL TALK TO THEM.

I'D LIKE A WORD WITH YOU, PLEASE, GENTLEMEN.
JUST ONE WORD? WHAT ABOUT A FIGHT AS WELL?

I CAN DO THAT, TOO, IF YOU GIVE ME A REASON.
CAN'T YOU FIND A REASON ON YOUR OWN?

MERCUTIO, YOU'RE IN ROMEO'S GROUP.
GROUP?
WHAT ARE WE? MUSICIANS? GIVE ME MY SWORD. I'LL MAKE YOU DANCE!

LET'S ARGUE SOMEWHERE ELSE. THERE ARE TOO MANY PEOPLE WATCHING US HERE.
CLUCK CLUCK

LET THEM WATCH! I'M NOT GOING ANYWHERE.
AH, HERE'S MY MAN!

HE'S NOT ONE OF YOUR MEN.

ROMEO, YOU **VILLAIN**!
I'LL **IGNORE** THAT. I'M NOT A **VILLAIN**.

SO, GOOD-BYE. YOU DON'T KNOW ME AT ALL.
BUT I WON'T **IGNORE** THE WAY YOU **INSULTED** ME!

I NEVER **INSULTED** YOU. YOU DON'T UNDERSTAND HOW MUCH I RESPECT THE CAPULET NAME.
IT'S NOT GOOD TO BACK DOWN LIKE THIS.

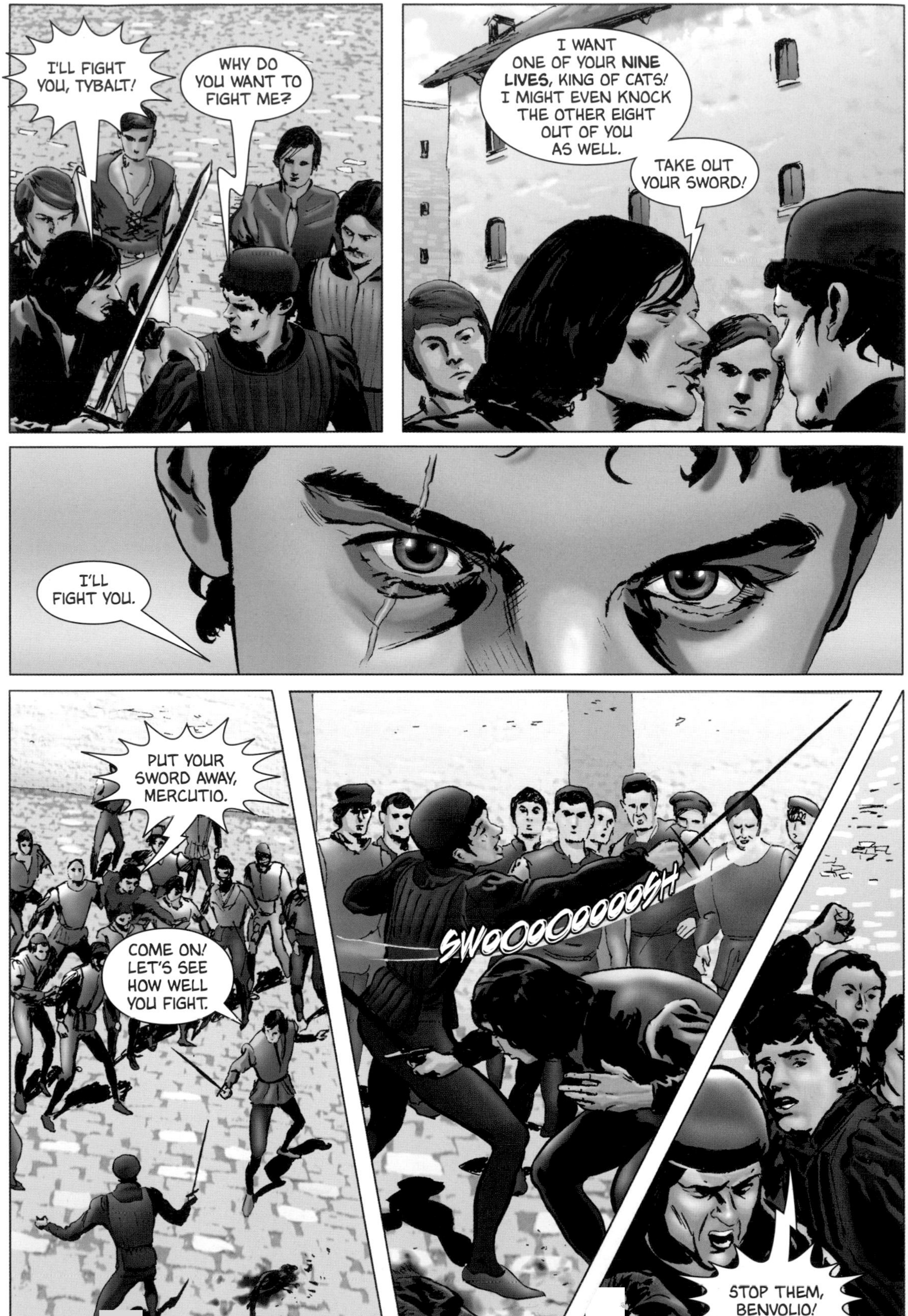

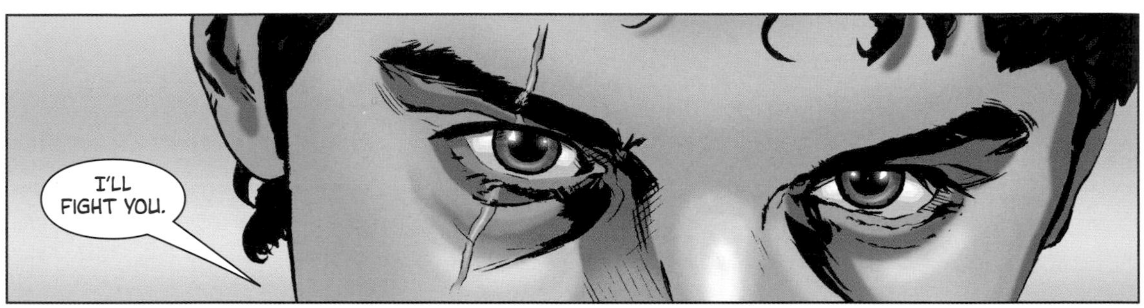

PUT YOUR SWORD AWAY, MERCUTIO.

COME ON! LET'S SEE HOW WELL YOU FIGHT.

SWOOOOOOOOOSH

STOP THEM, BENVOLIO!

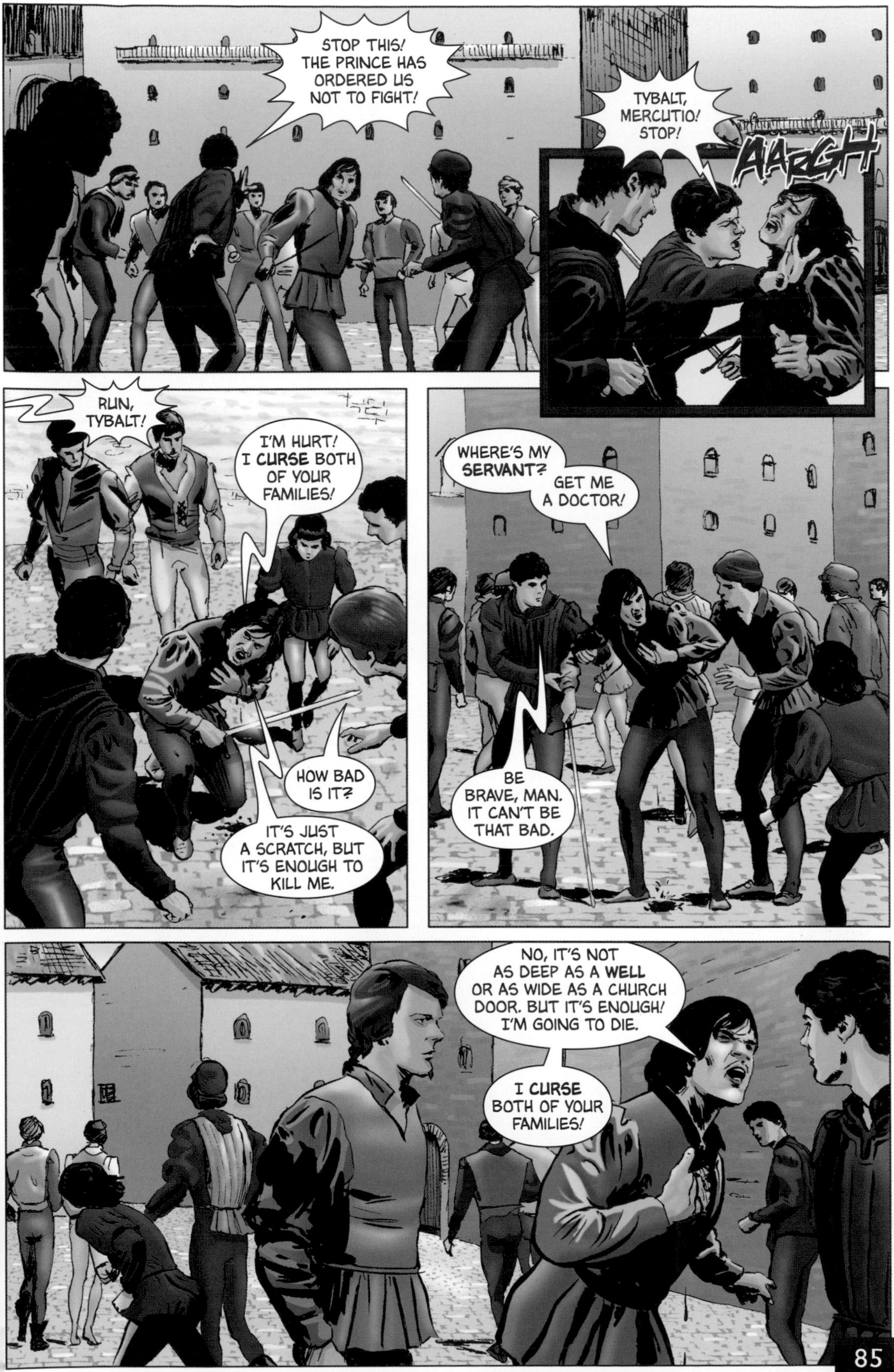

STOP THIS! THE PRINCE HAS ORDERED US NOT TO FIGHT!

TYBALT, MERCUTIO! STOP!

AARGH

RUN, TYBALT!

I'M HURT! I **CURSE** BOTH OF YOUR FAMILIES!

HOW BAD IS IT?

IT'S JUST A SCRATCH, BUT IT'S ENOUGH TO KILL ME.

WHERE'S MY **SERVANT**? GET ME A DOCTOR!

BE BRAVE, MAN. IT CAN'T BE THAT BAD.

Why did you get between us, Romeo? He stabbed me under your arm.
I WAS TRYING TO HELP –

Benvolio, get me into a house before I **faint**.

I **CURSE** BOTH OF YOUR FAMILIES!

YOUR FAMILIES HAVE KILLED ME!
MERCUTIO IS MY FRIEND AND A RELATIVE OF THE PRINCE. IT'S MY FAULT THAT HE'S BEEN HURT.
OH, JULIET, MY LOVE FOR YOU HAS MADE ME WEAK.

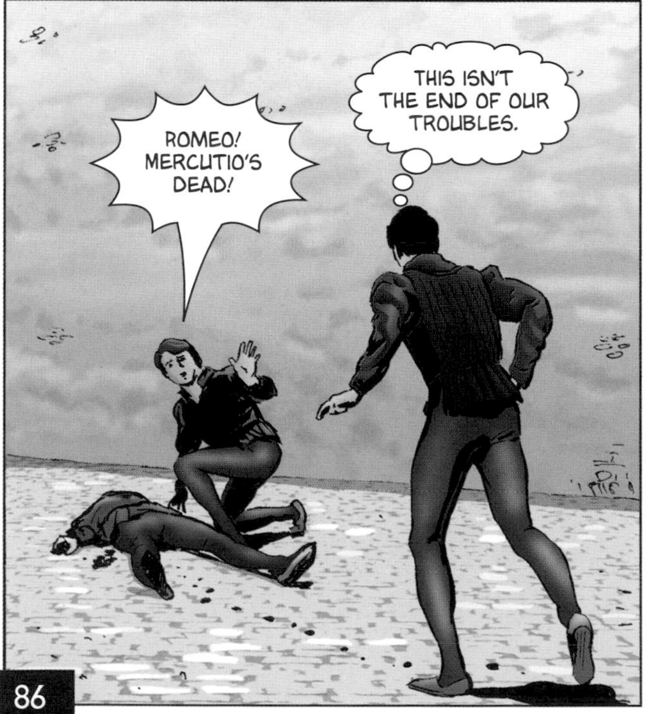
ROMEO! MERCUTIO'S DEAD!
THIS ISN'T THE END OF OUR TROUBLES.

HERE'S TYBALT AGAIN.
HE'S ALIVE, AND MERCUTIO'S DEAD!
I'M TOO ANGRY TO CONTROL MYSELF!

TYBALT, YOU'RE THE VILLAIN NOW!
ONE OF US WILL BE DYING WITH MERCUTIO TODAY.

YOU! YOU CAN JOIN HIM!
WE'LL SEE ABOUT THAT!

CLANG

AGHHK

THUD

GET OUT OF HERE, ROMEO!
TYBALT'S DEAD, AND THE OFFICERS ARE COMING. IF THEY CATCH YOU, YOU'LL BE EXECUTED.

I'M SUCH A FOOL!
GO!

WHICH WAY DID MERCUTIO'S KILLER, TYBALT, GO?

HE'S LYING OVER THERE.
YOU, COME WITH ME, BY ORDER OF THE PRINCE.

A FEW MINUTES LATER ...
WHO STARTED THIS FIGHT?

NOBLE PRINCE,
TYBALT KILLED MERCUTIO, AND THEN ROMEO KILLED TYBALT.

OH! MY NEPHEW, TYBALT, HAS BEEN KILLED!

OH, HE IS DEAD!
PLEASE, PRINCE, YOU HAVE TO MAKE A MONTAGUE PAY FOR THIS MURDER – WITH HIS LIFE!
OH, MY **NEPHEW!**

BENVOLIO, WHO STARTED THIS FIGHT?

TYBALT.

ROMEO TRIED TO STOP HIM, BUT TYBALT WOULDN'T LISTEN. HE TOOK OUT HIS SWORD AND POINTED IT AT MERCUTIO'S HEART.

MERCUTIO GOT ANGRY, AND THEN THEY BEGAN FIGHTING.
ROMEO TRIED TO BREAK IT UP AND GOT BETWEEN THEM.

TYBALT REACHED UNDER ROMEO'S ARM AND STABBED MERCUTIO. THEN TYBALT RAN AWAY.

ROMEO WANTED **REVENGE.** WHEN TYBALT CAME BACK, THEY BEGAN FIGHTING.
TYBALT WAS DEAD BEFORE I COULD GET BETWEEN THEM.
BANG BANG

THIS MAN IS A MONTAGUE! HE'S LYING TO PROTECT THEM.
IT TOOK TWENTY OF THEM TO KILL TYBALT!
I **DEMAND JUSTICE**, PRINCE. ROMEO HAS TO DIE!

ROMEO KILLED TYBALT BECAUSE TYBALT KILLED MERCUTIO. WHO WILL PAY FOR MERCUTIO'S LIFE?

NOT ROMEO, PRINCE. HE WAS MERCUTIO'S FRIEND.
WHEN HE KILLED TYBALT, HE WAS ONLY DOING WHAT THE LAW WOULD DO.

AND FOR DOING THAT HE HAS TO LEAVE VERONA IMMEDIATELY!
MERCUTIO WAS PART OF MY FAMILY. NOW, I HAVE BEEN **AFFECTED** BY YOUR FIGHTING.
YOU'LL ALL PAY DEARLY FOR THIS.

TELL ROMEO TO LEAVE THE CITY RIGHT AWAY.
IF HE IS SEEN HERE AGAIN, HE WILL BE **EXECUTED**.

Act III, Scene II
THE CAPULETS' HOUSE – MONDAY EVENING
I WISH THIS DAY WOULD END. I CAN'T WAIT FOR ROMEO TO BE IN MY ARMS.
THE DARKNESS OF NIGHT WILL MAKE SURE NO ONE SEES HIM COMING HERE.
I WANT TO WIN HIS HEART AND BE COMPLETELY HIS.
THE DARKNESS WILL HIDE MY EMBARASSMENT.
COME, NIGHT! COME, ROMEO! COME, LOVE!
GIVE ME MY ROMEO! AND, WHEN HE DIES, MAKE LITTLE STARS OUT OF HIM TO LIGHT UP THE NIGHT SKY. THAT WAY, THE WHOLE WORLD WILL BE IN LOVE WITH THE NIGHT.
I CAN'T WAIT FOR US TO BE TOGETHER.

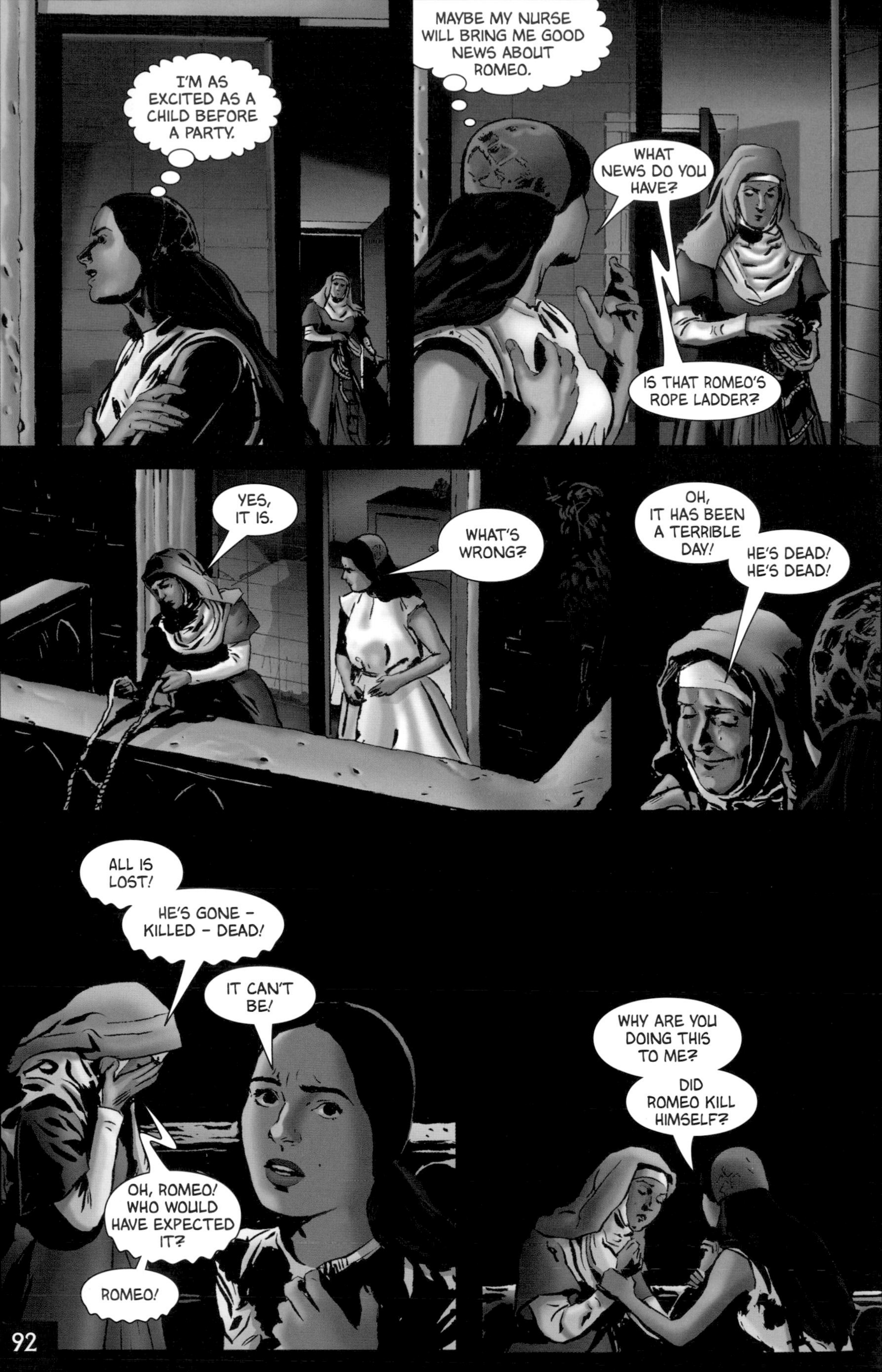

I'M AS EXCITED AS A CHILD BEFORE A PARTY.
MAYBE MY NURSE WILL BRING ME GOOD NEWS ABOUT ROMEO.
WHAT NEWS DO YOU HAVE?
IS THAT ROMEO'S ROPE LADDER?

ALL IS LOST!
HE'S GONE – KILLED – DEAD!
IT CAN'T BE!
OH, ROMEO! WHO WOULD HAVE EXPECTED IT?
ROMEO!
WHY ARE YOU DOING THIS TO ME?
DID ROMEO KILL HIMSELF?

IF YOU SAY "YES," THEN I WILL DIE, TOO.
IF HE'S DEAD, SAY "YES." IF NOT, SAY "NO."

I SAW HIM WITH MY OWN EYES.
HE WAS AS **PALE** AS ASHES AND COVERED IN BLOOD. I **FAINTED** WHEN I SAW HIM.

MY HEART IS BROKEN! I'LL KILL MYSELF!
OH, TYBALT! YOU WERE MY BEST FRIEND!

WHAT ARE YOU SAYING?
ARE TYBALT AND ROMEO BOTH DEAD?

ROMEO KILLED TYBALT, AND NOW ROMEO HAS BEEN **BANISHED** FROM VERONA.
OH, MY GOODNESS! ROMEO KILLED TYBALT?

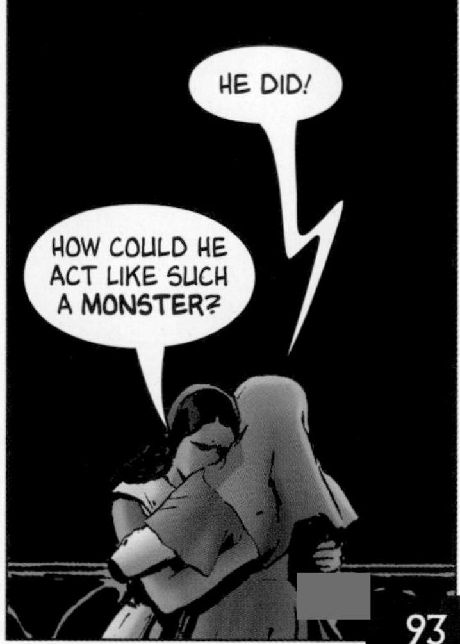
HE DID!
HOW COULD HE ACT LIKE SUCH A **MONSTER**?

HE SEEMED LIKE A GOOD MAN, BUT HE IS REALLY A **VILLAIN**.

HOW COULD A HORRIBLE BOOK HAVE SUCH A LOVELY COVER? HOW COULD NATURE MAKE SUCH A **MONSTER**?
NO MAN CAN BE TRUSTED.

WHERE'S PETER? I NEED A DRINK.
SHAME ON ROMEO!

NO. DON'T SAY THAT.
I KNOW THAT ROMEO IS REALLY A GOOD MAN. I KNOW IT!

OH, HOW COULD I HAVE SAID THOSE AWFUL THINGS ABOUT HIM?
HE KILLED YOUR COUSIN!

HE'S MY HUSBAND! I SHOULD STAND BY HIM.
BUT WHY DID HE KILL TYBALT?

TYBALT WOULD CERTAINLY HAVE KILLED MY HUSBAND!
I HAVE TO STOP CRYING. I SHOULD BE HAPPY THAT ROMEO IS ALIVE.

THAT IS GOOD NEWS, ISN'T IT?
THEN WHY AM I CRYING?
YOU SAID SOMETHING ELSE, NURSE. SOMETHING THAT MAKES ME WANT TO DIE.

I WISH I DIDN'T HEAR IT, BUT I CANNOT FORGET IT.
YOU SAID, "ROMEO IS **BANISHED.**"
THAT'S WORSE THAN THE DEATH OF TEN THOUSAND TYBALTS.
IT'S BAD ENOUGH THAT TYBALT IS DEAD. EVEN IF YOU'D SAID MY MOTHER AND FATHER WERE DEAD, TOO, THAT WOULD HAVE GIVEN ME A REASON TO BE SAD.

BUT, TO FOLLOW WITH "ROMEO IS **BANISHED**" IS LIKE SAYING MY FATHER AND MOTHER, TYBALT, ROMEO, AND JULIET ARE ALL DEAD.
NOTHING COULD BE WORSE!
WHERE ARE MY PARENTS, NURSE?
GRIEVING OVER TYBALT'S BODY.
I'LL TAKE YOU TO THEM.

WHEN ALL THEIR TEARS ARE DRY, I'LL STILL BE CRYING FOR ROMEO.
NURSE, TAKE THE ROPE LADDER AWAY.

WE DON'T NEED IT ANYMORE. WE HAVE BOTH LOST WHO WE WERE MADE FOR.
I'M GOING TO BED, WHERE DEATH, NOT ROMEO, WILL TAKE ME.

STAY IN YOUR ROOM. I KNOW WHERE ROMEO IS. I'LL GET HIM FOR YOU.
PLEASE FIND HIM AND GIVE HIM THIS RING. TELL HIM TO COME HERE AND SAY GOOD-BYE FOR THE LAST TIME.

Act III, Scene III
FRIAR LAURENCE'S CHURCH – MONDAY NIGHT
COME OUT, ROMEO.
YOU ALWAYS SEEM TO BE IN TROUBLE.
DO YOU HAVE ANY NEWS, **FRIAR** LAURENCE?

I HAVE NEWS ABOUT THE PRINCE'S PUNISHMENT.

AM I GOING TO BE **EXECUTED?**

NO. THE **SENTENCE** WAS **BANISHMENT.**
BANISHMENT?
THAT'S EVEN WORSE THAN DEATH!

YOU'RE ONLY **BANISHED** FROM VERONA. THE WORLD IS A BIG PLACE.

THERE IS NO WORLD OUTSIDE VERONA! BANISHMENT IS JUST DEATH BY ANOTHER NAME.
IT'S THE SAME AS KILLING ME.
HOW UNGRATEFUL! WHAT YOU DID IS PUNISHABLE BY DEATH. BUT THE PRINCE HAS BANISHED YOU INSTEAD,
AND YOU'RE NOT HAPPY.

HE HASN'T SHOWN ME ANY MERCY.
I WANT TO BE HERE, WHERE JULIET IS.

EVERY LIVING CREATURE UNDER THE SUN CAN STAY IN VERONA AND BE WITH JULIET –
EXCEPT ME!

AND YOU SAY BANISHMENT IS BETTER THAN DEATH?

KILL ME
WITH SOMETHING
ELSE BESIDES
BANISHMENT!

HOW CAN
YOU EVEN SAY THAT
HORRIBLE WORD
TO ME?
"BANISHMENT!"
SMAAASH

LISTEN
TO ME.
NO! YOU'LL
ONLY TALK ABOUT
BANISHMENT.

I CAN GIVE
YOU ADVICE THAT
WILL HELP YOU.
CAN YOUR
ADVICE CREATE ANOTHER
JULIET, OR MOVE A CITY,
OR REVERSE A PRINCE'S
SENTENCE?
IF IT CAN'T,
THEN I DON'T WANT
TO HEAR IT.

CRAZY
MEN NEVER
LISTEN.
AND WISE
MEN CANNOT
SEE!
LET ME
SPEAK!

YOU CAN'T TALK ABOUT SOMETHING THAT YOU DON'T UNDERSTAND!
YOU'RE NOT YOUNG AND IN LOVE LIKE I AM!

KNOCK KNOCK
GET UP. SOMEONE'S KNOCKING.
HIDE!

NO. LET THE MISTY BREATH FROM MY BROKEN HEART HIDE ME.
KNOCK KNOCK
THEY'RE STILL KNOCKING!

KNOCK KNOCK
WHO'S THERE?

ROMEO, GET UP!
YOU'LL GET ARRESTED!

KNOCK KNOCK
WAIT!

HIDE IN MY STUDY.

KNOCK KNOCK
JUST A MINUTE!

HURRY!

KNOCK KNOCK KNOCK KNOCK
WHO IS IT? WHAT DO YOU WANT?
LET ME IN. LADY JULIET SENT ME.

THEN YOU ARE WELCOME HERE.
WHERE'S ROMEO?

LYING ON THE GROUND, CRYING.
HE'S ACTING JUST LIKE JULIET!
THIS IS SO SAD!

SHE'S ACTING JUST LIKE THIS – BLUBBERING AND CRYING.
STAND UP AND BE A MAN! GET UP FOR JULIET'S SAKE!
NURSE!

YOU CAN'T JUST LIE THERE!
HOW IS JULIET? WHERE IS SHE? WHAT DID SHE SAY WHEN SHE HEARD ABOUT ME?

SHE SAID NOTHING. SHE JUST CRIED AND CALLED OUT "TYBALT" AND "ROMEO."

IT'S ALL MY FAULT!

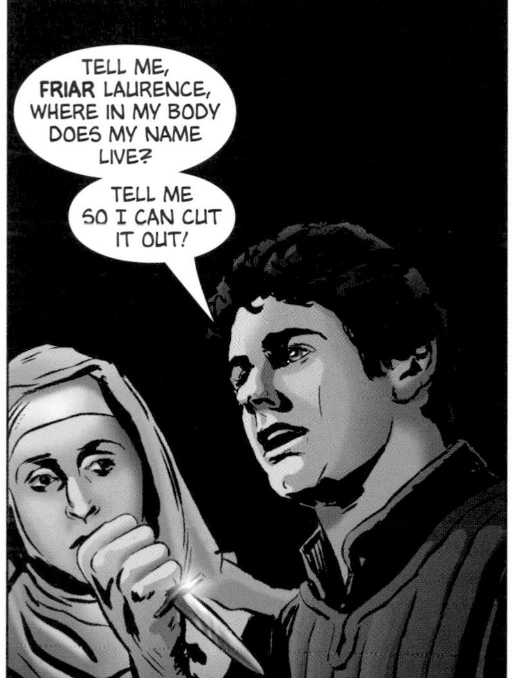
TELL ME, **FRIAR** LAURENCE, WHERE IN MY BODY DOES MY NAME LIVE?
TELL ME SO I CAN CUT IT OUT!

DON'T DO IT!
COME ON, ACT LIKE A MAN!

I THOUGHT YOU WERE MORE **SENSIBLE** THAN THIS.
BY KILLING YOURSELF, YOU'LL ALSO BE KILLING YOUR WIFE - BECAUSE YOU ARE HER REASON FOR LIVING.

YOU SHOULD BE **ASHAMED** OF YOURSELF FOR EVEN THINKING ABOUT IT.

YOUR BODY IS LIKE A WAX MODEL – IT DOESN'T HOLD THE **SPIRIT** OF A REAL MAN.
YOU LIED WHEN YOU PROMISED TO LOVE YOUR WIFE. NOW YOUR MIND HAS TURNED AGAINST YOU.

LOOK AT WHAT YOU'VE GOT. JULIET IS ALIVE, AND SO ARE YOU.
TYBALT TRIED TO KILL YOU, AND YOU SHOULD HAVE BEEN **EXECUTED**.
YOU'RE A LUCKY MAN!

BUT HERE YOU ARE, COMPLAINING LIKE A CHILD.
PEOPLE WHO DO THAT USUALLY DIE SAD AND LONELY.

GO TO JULIET, LIKE WE PLANNED. BUT DON'T STAY TOO LONG OR THE TOWN GUARDS WILL STOP YOU FROM ESCAPING TO MANTUA.
THAT'S WHERE YOU HAVE TO LIVE UNTIL WE CAN FIGURE ALL THIS OUT AND BRING YOU BACK HERE AGAIN.

GO ON AHEAD OF HIM, NURSE. SEND MY **REGARDS** TO JULIET AND TELL HER ROMEO IS COMING.
YOU'RE A WONDERFUL MAN, **FRIAR** LAURENCE.
ROMEO, I'LL TELL JULIET THAT YOU'RE COMING.

PLEASE DO.
AND TELL HER THAT I UNDERSTAND IF SHE IS ANGRY AT ME.
SHE ASKED ME TO GIVE YOU THIS RING.
PLEASE HURRY. IT'S GETTING LATE.

THIS MAKES ME FEEL SO MUCH BETTER!

LEAVE BEFORE THE GUARDS GO ON DUTY OR WEAR A DISGUISE.
STAY IN MANTUA. YOUR **SERVANT** WILL UPDATE YOU WITH ANY NEWS FROM HERE.

IT'S LATE.
GOOD-BYE! GOOD NIGHT!
I'D BE SAD TO LEAVE IF I WASN'T GOING TO JULIET.
GOOD-BYE.

Act III, Scene IV

THE CAPULETS' HOUSE – MONDAY NIGHT
WITH ALL THAT'S BEEN GOING ON, WE HAVEN'T HAD TIME TO **CONVINCE** JULIET TO MARRY YOU.
SHE REALLY LOVED TYBALT, AND SO DID I.
IT'S LATE NOW. SHE WON'T COME DOWN TONIGHT.

I UNDERSTAND.
GOOD NIGHT, **MADAM**. GIVE MY **REGARDS** TO JULIET.
I WILL.

WAIT! COUNT PARIS, I WILL ACCEPT YOUR MARRIAGE PROPOSAL FOR MY DAUGHTER.
I'M SURE SHE'LL AGREE WITH MY DECISION.

LET'S HAVE THE WEDDING ON WEDNESDAY.
WAIT ... WHAT DAY IS IT TODAY?
MONDAY.

MONDAY? THEN WEDNESDAY IS TOO SOON. MAKE IT THURSDAY.
WILL YOU BE READY? WE'LL JUST INVITE A FEW FRIENDS.

IT WOULD BE WRONG FOR US TO HAVE A BIG PARTY SO SOON AFTER TYBALT'S DEATH.
HOW DO YOU FEEL ABOUT HAVING THE WEDDING ON THURSDAY?

I WISH THURSDAY WAS TOMORROW.
THEN THURSDAY IT IS.

GO TO JULIET, DEAR WIFE. MAKE SURE SHE IS READY TO GET MARRIED.

GOOD-BYE, COUNT PARIS.

LIGHT THE WAY TO MY BEDROOM! IT'S SO LATE. IT'S GOING TO BE MORNING SOON!

Act III, Scene V
THE CAPULETS' HOUSE, JULIET'S ROOM - EARLY TUESDAY MORNING
DO YOU HAVE TO GO?
IT'S NOT MORNING YET. THAT WAS THE NIGHTINGALE YOU HEARD, NOT THE LARK.

LOOK, MY LOVE, IT'S **DAWN**. IT'S ALMOST DAY.
I HAVE TO GO OR I'LL BE KILLED.

THAT'S NOT **DAWN**. IT'S PROBABLY SOME **METEOR** THAT HAS COME TO LIGHT YOUR WAY TO MANTUA.
STAY A LITTLE BIT LONGER.

IF THAT'S WHAT YOU WANT, I DON'T CARE IF I GET ARRESTED AND **EXECUTED**.
I'LL PRETEND IT ISN'T MORNING. I HAVE MORE REASONS TO STAY THAN I HAVE TO LEAVE.

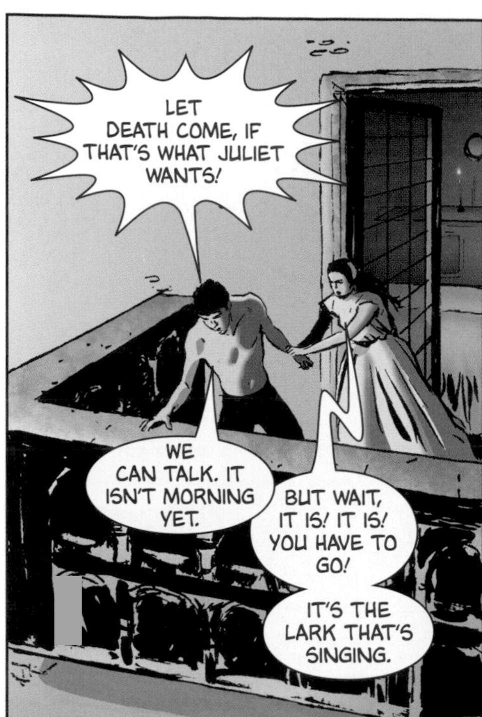
LET DEATH COME, IF THAT'S WHAT JULIET WANTS!
WE CAN TALK. IT ISN'T MORNING YET.
BUT WAIT, IT IS! IT IS! YOU HAVE TO GO!
IT'S THE LARK THAT'S SINGING.

FROM NOW ON, I'LL HATE THE SOUND OF THE LARK BECAUSE IT'S TEARING US APART.

PLEASE LEAVE! IT'S GETTING BRIGHTER.
AND OUR SADNESS IS GROWING DARKER.
MADAM!

NURSE?
WATCH OUT. YOUR MOTHER'S COMING!
AND MY LIFE IS GOING!

GOOD-BYE!
ONE KISS, AND I'LL LEAVE.

YOU'RE GONE ALREADY? MY HUSBAND, MY LOVE, MY FRIEND!
IT'S GOING TO FEEL LIKE SUCH A LONG TIME UNTIL I GET TO SEE MY ROMEO AGAIN.

GOOD-BYE! I WILL SEND MY LOVE TO YOU WHENEVER I CAN.
WILL WE EVER SEE EACH OTHER AGAIN?
OF COURSE WE WILL!

OH! I HAVE A BAD FEELING. SEEING YOU DOWN THERE, YOU ARE LIKE A DEAD MAN IN A **GRAVE**. YOU LOOK SO **PALE**.
SADNESS HAS MADE US BOTH **PALE**. GOOD-BYE!

FORTUNE HAS SENT YOU AWAY QUICKLY, BUT MAYBE IT CAN SEND YOU BACK TO ME JUST AS QUICKLY.

JULIET, ARE YOU AWAKE?
IS THAT MY MOTHER?
WHAT CAN SHE WANT AT THIS HOUR?

HOW ARE YOU, JULIET?
NOT VERY WELL.
ARE YOU STILL CRYING FOR TYBALT?

YOU MAY WASH HIM FROM HIS **GRAVE** WITH ALL YOUR TEARS, BUT IT WON'T BRING HIM BACK TO LIFE.
SO STOP NOW.
LET ME CRY FOR MY LOSS.

HE'S GONE.
I'LL CRY OVER HIM FOREVER.

PERHAPS YOU'RE CRYING BECAUSE THAT **VILLAIN** IS STILL ALIVE.
WHAT **VILLAIN**?
ROMEO.

HE ISN'T A **VILLAIN**.

GOD FORGIVE HIM!
I FORGIVE HIM, BUT THERE ISN'T ANOTHER MAN WHO UPSETS ME MORE.
THAT'S BECAUSE HE'S STILL ALIVE.

YES, AND BECAUSE HE'S OUT OF MY REACH.
WE'LL HAVE OUR **REVENGE**, DON'T WORRY.
I'LL GET SOMEONE IN MANTUA TO **POISON** HIM. WILL THAT **SATISFY** YOU?

I WON'T BE **SATISFIED** UNTIL I SEE ROMEO - DEAD. MY HEART IS BROKEN BY MY COUSIN'S DEATH.
I WILL MIX THE **POISON** MYSELF SO THAT ROMEO WILL SLEEP DEEPLY WHEN HE TAKES IT.

I WANT TO BE NEAR ROMEO. I WANT TO **INFLICT** THE LOVE I HAD FOR TYBALT ON THE BODY OF THE MAN WHO KILLED HIM.
WE'LL FIND A WAY. BUT NOW I HAVE SOME HAPPY NEWS FOR YOU.

GOOD! I COULD USE SOME HAPPINESS.
YOUR FATHER HAS ARRANGED A SURPRISE – TO TAKE YOUR MIND OFF YOUR **SORROW**.

WHEN WILL I GET IT?

ON THURSDAY MORNING. YOU'LL BE MARRIED TO COUNT PARIS AT ST. PETER'S CHURCH.

NO! I WON'T MARRY HIM!
I DON'T EVEN KNOW HIM.
TELL MY FATHER I'M NOT READY TO GET MARRIED YET –

- AND, WHEN I DO, IT WON'T BE TO COUNT PARIS. I'D RATHER MARRY ROMEO -
- WHOM I HATE.
HERE COMES YOUR FATHER. YOU CAN TELL HIM YOURSELF.

WHAT'S GOING ON? ARE YOU STILL CRYING, GIRL?

YOUR EYES ARE LIKE LITTLE BOATS BEING TOSSED ABOUT ON A SEA OF TEARS.

DID YOU TELL HER?
I DID, BUT SHE WON'T AGREE TO IT. I WISH THIS FOOLISH GIRL WAS DEAD!

WHAT DO YOU MEAN? SHE WON'T AGREE TO IT?
ISN'T SHE GRATEFUL THAT WE HAVE ARRANGED SUCH A GOOD MARRIAGE FOR HER?
I AM GRATEFUL, BUT -

BUT WHAT?
"THANKS, BUT NO THANKS"?
YOU STILL LIVE UNDER MY ROOF! YOU'LL BE IN ST. PETER'S CHURCH NEXT THURSDAY, EVEN IF I HAVE TO DRAG YOU THERE MYSELF!
I'M **ASHAMED** OF YOU, YOU LITTLE BRAT.
CRASH

WHAT ARE YOU DOING? ARE YOU CRAZY?
DEAR FATHER, PLEASE!
LET ME SPEAK –

YOU ARE WORTHLESS AND DISOBEDIENT!

IF YOU DON'T MARRY COUNT PARIS ON THURSDAY, I NEVER WANT TO SEE YOU AGAIN.
DON'T TALK BACK TO ME, OR I'LL HIT YOU!

WE THOUGHT WE WERE UNLUCKY FOR ONLY HAVING ONE CHILD. BUT NOW I SEE THAT THIS ONE IS ONE TOO MANY!
YOU'RE WRONG TO SAY THAT ABOUT JULIET.

BE QUIET!
I CAN'T SPEAK EITHER?

YOU CAN SPEAK WHEN YOU'RE WITH YOUR **GOSSIPING** FRIENDS.
YOU'RE TOO ANGRY.
THIS MAKES ME ANGRY!

ALL I'VE EVER WANTED FOR HER WAS A GOOD HUSBAND.
AND NOW THAT I'VE FOUND THE PERFECT MAN –

– I HAVE TO LISTEN TO HER **WHINING**,
"I WON'T MARRY HIM, I DON'T LOVE HIM, I'M TOO YOUNG."
IF YOU DON'T MARRY COUNT PARIS, YOU CAN LEAVE THIS HOUSE!

I'M NOT JOKING!
YOU'LL MARRY COUNT PARIS, OR YOU WON'T BE MY DAUGHTER ANYMORE.
AND YOU CAN **STARVE** IN THE STREETS FOR ALL I CARE.

DOESN'T HEAVEN HAVE ANY **PITY** FOR ME?
CAN'T IT SEE MY **GRIEF**?
OH, MOTHER, DON'T LEAVE ME! DELAY THIS MARRIAGE, OR I'LL DIE.
DO WHATEVER YOU WANT. I'M FINISHED WITH YOU.

OH, NURSE! HOW DO WE STOP THIS?

ROMEO IS MY HUSBAND, AND HE'S STILL ALIVE. I CANNOT MARRY COUNT PARIS.

PLEASE SAY SOMETHING TO **COMFORT** ME!
ALL RIGHT!
ROMEO IS **BANISHED** AND IS PROBABLY NOT GOING TO RETURN TO VERONA.
SO I THINK IT'S BEST THAT YOU MARRY COUNT PARIS.

HE'S A LOVELY MAN! ROMEO IS NOTHING COMPARED TO HIM.
JUST THINK OF ROMEO AS IF HE IS DEAD.

IS THAT REALLY WHAT YOU THINK?
IT IS WHAT I THINK IN MY HEART AND IN MY **SOUL**, TOO. OR **CURSE** THEM BOTH.
AMEN!
WHAT?

YOU HAVE GIVEN ME **COMFORT**.
TELL MY MOTHER THAT I'VE GONE TO **FRIAR** LAURENCE TO ASK FORGIVENESS FOR MAKING MY FATHER ANGRY.
IT'S THE RIGHT THING TO DO.

WICKED OLD WITCH! I'LL NEVER TRUST HER WITH MY SECRETS AGAIN.
FRIAR LAURENCE WILL KNOW WHAT TO DO. IF NOTHING ELSE WORKS, I CAN ALWAYS KILL MYSELF.

Act IV, Scene I
FRIAR LAURENCE'S CHURCH – TUESDAY MORNING
ON THURSDAY, SIR? THAT'S VERY SOON.
THAT'S WHEN LORD CAPULET WANTS IT.
BUT YOU DON'T KNOW WHAT JULIET THINKS YET.

SHE IS STILL GRIEVING OVER TYBALT, AND I HAVEN'T BEEN ABLE TO TALK TO HER.

HER FATHER THINKS IT'S DANGEROUS FOR HER TO BE SO UNHAPPY.
HE THINKS WE SHOULD GET MARRIED QUICKLY TO MAKE HER HAPPY AGAIN. NOW YOU KNOW WHY WE NEED TO HURRY.
AND I ALSO KNOW WHY IT SHOULD BE DELAYED.

HERE COMES JULIET.
grasp

I'M HAPPY TO SEE YOU, MY LADY AND MY WIFE!
I'M NOT YOUR WIFE YET.
YOU WILL BE ON THURSDAY.
WHAT WILL BE, WILL BE.
VERY TRUE.

HAVE YOU COME TO MAKE **CONFESSION** TO **FRIAR** LARENCE?
TO HIM, NOT YOU!

TELL HIM THAT YOU LOVE ME.
I'LL TELL YOU THAT I LOVE HIM.

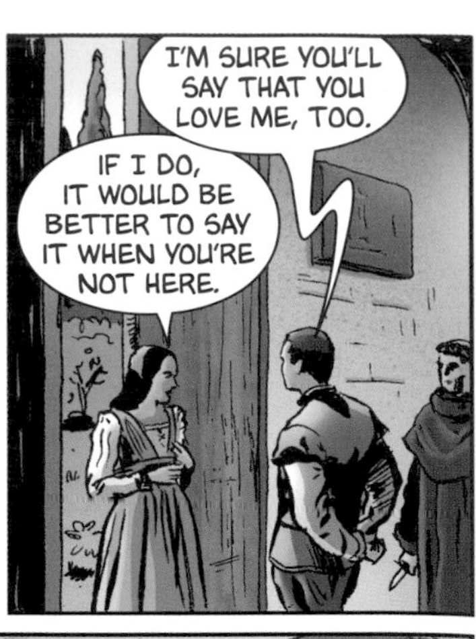
I'M SURE YOU'LL SAY THAT YOU LOVE ME, TOO.
IF I DO, IT WOULD BE BETTER TO SAY IT WHEN YOU'RE NOT HERE.

YOUR FACE LOOKS LIKE YOU HAVE BEEN CRYING.
IT ALWAYS LOOKS THIS WAY.

NO. DON'T SAY THAT!
IT'S THE TRUTH.
YOUR FACE IS MINE, AND YOU ARE **INSULTING** IT.

THAT MAY BE TRUE SINCE MY FACE ISN'T MINE ANYMORE.

DO YOU HAVE TIME NOW, **FRIAR** LAURENCE, OR SHOULD I COME BACK LATER?
I HAVE TIME NOW.

PLEASE EXCUSE US.
OF COURSE.

JULIET, I'LL COME FOR YOU EARLY ON THURSDAY MORNING.
GOOD-BYE, UNTIL THEN.

PLEASE SHUT THE DOOR!
I HAVE NO HOPE!

I HAVE HEARD. YOU ARE GOING TO MARRY COUNT PARIS ON THURSDAY.

TELL ME HOW I CAN STOP IT!
IF YOU CAN'T, I DON'T WANT TO LIVE ANYMORE!

I'M MARRIED TO ROMEO!
I'LL KILL MYSELF BEFORE I'LL MARRY ANYONE ELSE.
PLEASE TELL ME WHAT TO DO!

GIVE ME AN ANSWER!
I WANT TO DIE IF THERE'S NO OTHER WAY OUT.
STOP THIS!

I HAVE AN IDEA, BUT IT'S VERY DANGEROUS.
IF YOU'RE WILLING TO DIE, THEN PERHAPS YOU WOULD DO SOMETHING THAT IS LIKE DYING TO SOLVE THIS PROBLEM.

WOULD YOU?
I WOULD DO ANYTHING TO GET OUT OF MARRYING COUNT PARIS!

ANYTHING TO BE ABLE TO LIVE AS A **FAITHFUL** WIFE TO MY SWEET LOVE!

ALL RIGHT, THEN. GO HOME AND LOOK HAPPY. AGREE TO MARRY COUNT PARIS.
MAKE SURE YOU ARE ALONE TOMORROW NIGHT AND DRINK THIS WHEN YOU GO TO BED.

YOU WILL FALL INTO A DEEP, DEEP SLEEP. YOUR HEART WILL STOP BEATING, YOUR BODY WILL GO COLD, AND YOU WILL STOP BREATHING.
YOU'LL LOOK LIKE YOU'RE DEAD.

THIS WILL LAST FOR FORTY-TWO HOURS. THEN YOU WILL WAKE UP AND RETURN TO NORMAL.

WHEN COUNT PARIS COMES TO GET YOU, EVERYONE WILL THINK YOU'RE DEAD.
YOU'LL BE TAKEN TO THE CAPULET **TOMB** AND **LAID TO REST** THERE.
IN THE MEANTIME, I'LL WRITE TO ROMEO AND TELL HIM WHAT'S GOING ON.
WE'LL BOTH BE IN THE **TOMB** WHEN YOU WAKE UP. THEN HE WILL TAKE YOU WITH HIM TO MANTUA.
ARE YOU SURE YOU WANT TO DO THIS?
GIVE IT TO ME!
BE STRONG. I'LL SEND A **FRIAR** TO MANTUA WITH A LETTER FOR ROMEO.
LOVE WILL GIVE ME STRENGTH!
GOOD-BYE, **FRIAR** LAURENCE!

Act IV, Scene II

THE CAPULETS' HOUSE – TUESDAY EVENING
INVITE EVERYONE ON THIS LIST.

GET ME TWENTY GOOD COOKS.
I WILL ASK THEM TO LICK THEIR FINGERS.

WHY?
IF A COOK WON'T LICK HIS OWN FINGERS, HE'S NOT VERY GOOD.
HURRY! WE DON'T HAVE MUCH TIME.

DID JULIET GO TO FRIAR LAURENCE?
YES.
WELL, I HOPE HE CAN MAKE THAT **STUBBORN** GIRL BE **SENSIBLE**.

HERE SHE COMES.
WHERE HAVE YOU BEEN?

FRIAR LAURENCE TOLD ME TO BEG YOU FOR FORGIVENESS.
PLEASE FORGIVE ME. I'M READY TO DO WHATEVER YOU WANT.

SEND FOR COUNT PARIS.
WE WILL HAVE THE WEDDING TOMORROW MORNING!

I MET COUNT PARIS AT **FRIAR** LAURENCE'S CHURCH, AND I GAVE HIM MY LOVING RESPECT.

THIS IS GOOD. THIS IS HOW IT SHOULD BE!

BRING COUNT PARIS HERE.
WE OWE THIS **FRIAR** A LOT.

NURSE, WILL YOU HELP ME CHOOSE MY CLOTHES?
THERE'S PLENTY OF TIME BEFORE THURSDAY.
THE WEDDING IS TOMORROW!

WE WON'T BE READY IN TIME!
I'LL WORK EVERYTHING OUT, EVEN IF I HAVE TO STAY UP ALL NIGHT.
YOU GO WITH JULIET.

WHERE DID EVERYONE GO? OH, WELL, I'LL VISIT COUNT PARIS MYSELF AND MAKE SURE HE IS READY FOR TOMORROW.

Act IV, Scene III

THE CAPULETS' HOUSE, JULIET'S ROOM - TUESDAY NIGHT

PLEASE, NURSE, I WANT TO BE ALONE TONIGHT. I NEED TO PRAY.

DO YOU NEED MY HELP?

NO, MOTHER. I'D LIKE TO BE ALONE NOW.

LET THE NURSE HELP YOU TONIGHT. I'M SURE YOU HAVE A LOT TO DO.

GOOD NIGHT.
GOOD-BYE!
GOD KNOWS WHEN WE'LL MEET AGAIN. I FEEL A COLD SHIVER.
NURSE!
NO. I HAVE TO DO THIS ALONE.

WHAT IF THIS DOESN'T WORK?
THEN I'LL HAVE TO USE THIS.
WHAT IF FRIAR LAURENCE GAVE ME POISON BECAUSE HE THINKS HE'LL GET IN TROUBLE FOR MARRYING ME TO ROMEO?
NO, FRIAR LAURENCE IS A GOOD MAN. HE WOULDN'T DO THAT.
BUT WHAT IF I WAKE UP BEFORE ROMEO GETS TO THE TOMB? I'LL SUFFOCATE BEFORE HE CAN SAVE ME!
EVEN IF I LIVE, I'LL BE SURROUNDED BY DEATH AND DARKNESS.
I'LL BE BURIED ALIVE NEXT TO MY ANCESTORS AND TYBALT.

OH, NO! I'LL WAKE UP TOO SOON AND BE SURROUNDED BY GHOSTS! I'LL GO CRAZY!
I'LL LOSE MY MIND AND PLAY WITH SKELETONS!
I'LL DRAG TYBALT FROM HIS GRAVE AND BASH OUT MY BRAINS WITH AN OLD BONE!
IS THAT TYBALT'S GHOST, LOOKING FOR ROMEO? STAY THERE, TYBALT!
I'M COMING, ROMEO!
I'M DRINKING THIS FOR YOU!

Act IV, Scene IV

THE CAPULETS' HOUSE – EARLY WEDNESDAY MORNING

GET MORE SPICES, NURSE.

THEY'RE SHOUTING FOR INGREDIENTS IN THE KITCHEN.

COME ON, GO FASTER!

IT'S THREE O'CLOCK!

GO TO BED, OR YOU'LL BE SICK TOMORROW.
NO, I WON'T! I'VE STAYED UP ALL NIGHT BEFORE.

OH, YES, YOU KNEW HOW TO PARTY WHEN YOU WERE YOUNGER. BUT I'M KEEPING AN EYE ON YOU NOW!
YOU'RE JEALOUS!

WHAT DO YOU HAVE THERE?
THINGS FOR THE COOK, SIR.

HURRY! HURRY!

GET SOME MORE LOGS. PETER WILL SHOW YOU WHERE THEY ARE.
I CAN FIND THE LOGS MYSELF.

THEN YOU'RE A LOG HEAD!

GOODNESS, IT'S MORNING ALREADY! COUNT PARIS WILL BE HERE SOON.
I HEAR HIM!
NURSE! WIFE!

GO WAKE UP JULIET AND GET HER DRESSED.
HURRY! THE **GROOM** IS HERE.

Act IV, Scene V

THE CAPULETS' HOUSE, JULIET'S ROOM - WEDNESDAY MORNING
KNOCK KNOCK KNOCK
Juliet! Sound asleep, I bet.
SWEETHEART!
BRIDE!

THAT'S RIGHT, GET ALL THE SLEEP YOU CAN! YOU WON'T BE GETTING MUCH REST TONIGHT!
SHE'S STILL SLEEPING - I'LL HAVE TO WAKE HER UP.

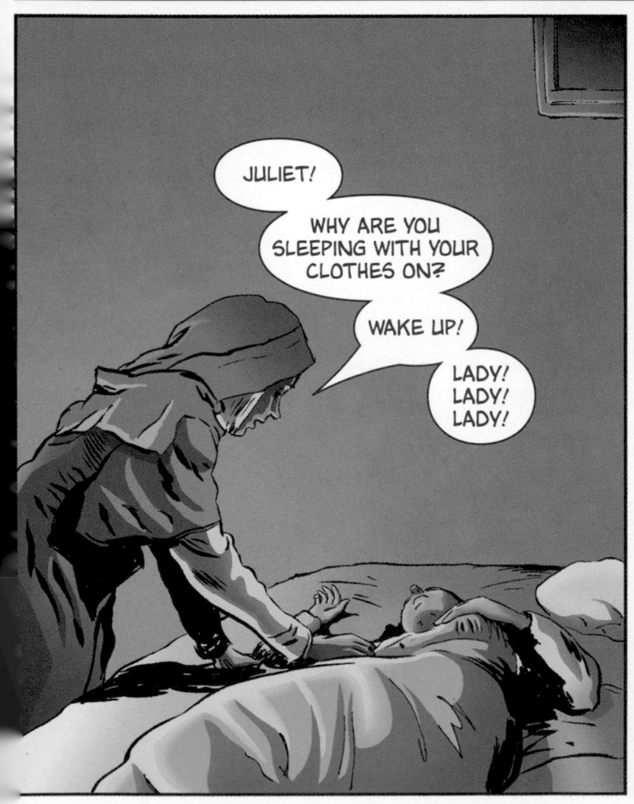

JULIET!
WHY ARE YOU SLEEPING WITH YOUR CLOTHES ON?
WAKE UP!
LADY! LADY! LADY!

OH, MY!
HELP!
MY LADY IS DEAD!
MY LORD! MY LADY!

WHAT'S THE MATTER?
OH, WHAT A TERRIBLE DAY!
WHAT'S WRONG?
LOOK!

OH, MY CHILD, MY LIFE! WAKE UP AND OPEN YOUR EYES.
HELP, HELP!

FOR GOODNESS SAKE, BRING JULIET DOWN. COUNT PARIS IS HERE.
SHE'S DEAD!
DEAD!

SHE'S DEAD,
SHE'S DEAD, SHE'S DEAD!

LET ME SEE HER.
OH, NO, SHE'S COLD! SHE HAS BEEN DEAD FOR SOME TIME.

OH, NO!
THIS IS HORRIBLE!
I DON'T KNOW WHAT TO SAY.

IS THE BRIDE READY TO GO TO CHURCH?

READY TO GO, BUT NEVER TO RETURN.
COUNT PARIS, YOUR BRIDE HAS DIED ON THE NIGHT BEFORE YOUR WEDDING DAY.

MY DAUGHTER IS MARRIED TO DEATH. DEATH IS MY NEW SON-IN-LAW AND MY ONLY HEIR.
I HAVE LOOKED FORWARD TO THIS MORNING, BUT NOW THIS IS WHAT'S HAPPENED!

WHAT A TERRIBLE DAY!
I ONLY HAD ONE CHILD. SHE WAS MY ONLY SOURCE OF HAPPINESS AND HOPE.
AND NOW CRUEL DEATH HAS TAKEN HER AWAY FROM ME.

WHAT A MISERABLE, MISERABLE DAY!
WHAT A DARK, TERRIBLE DAY!

I HAVE BEEN TRICKED - DIVORCED, WRONGED, AND HARMED - BY DEATH!
OH, MY LOVE! MY LIFE! YOU ARE GONE! BUT YOU ARE STILL MY LOVE IN DEATH!

WHY DID THIS HAPPEN?
WHY DID DEATH **RUIN** OUR PLANS?
OH, MY CHILD! MY CHILD IS DEAD! AND ALL MY HOPES AND DREAMS ARE DEAD WITH HER.

QUIET! CALM DOWN!
THIS SCREAMING AND CRYING ISN'T GOING TO HELP. JULIET HAS GONE TO HEAVEN. SHE WILL LIVE FOREVER.

SHE'S IN A BETTER PLACE. IT'S BETTER THAN THE LIFE YOU HAD PLANNED FOR HER HERE ON EARTH.
YOU CRY, BUT SHE'S PERFECTLY FINE UP THERE.

DRY YOUR TEARS AND WE'LL TAKE HER TO THE CHURCH.
I KNOW IT'S NATURAL TO **GRIEVE**, BUT YOU REALLY SHOULD BE HAPPY FOR HER.

THE WEDDING CELEBRATIONS HAVE TURNED INTO A SAD **FUNERAL**.
EVERYTHING IS THE OPPOSITE OF WHAT IT WAS.

HEAVEN IS ALREADY ANGRY. DON'T MAKE THINGS WORSE BY GOING AGAINST WHAT GOD WANTS.
EVERYONE, PREPARE FOR THE **FUNERAL**.

WE MIGHT AS WELL LEAVE.
PUT YOUR INSTRUMENTS AWAY. THEY'RE NOT NEEDED HERE.
YES, THIS IS A BAD DAY.

MUSICIANS, PLEASE PLAY "HEART'S EASE."
WHY?

I NEED A CHEERFULLY SAD SONG TO **COMFORT** ME.
NOW IS NOT THE TIME TO PLAY.

YOU WON'T PLAY?
NO.

THEN I'LL GIVE IT TO YOU.
WHAT WILL YOU GIVE US?
NO MONEY, JUST AN **INSULT**! I'LL CALL YOU A **MINSTREL**!
THEN I'LL CALL YOU A **SERVANT**!

THEN I'LL HIT YOU ON THE HEAD WITH MY KNIFE AND MAKE YOU SING. DO YOU HEAR ME?
OH, YOU'LL HEAR US SING ALL RIGHT!
PUT YOUR KNIFE AWAY, YOU FOOL.

I'M NOT A FOOL! ANSWER THIS QUESTION.
WHEN SADNESS HURTS YOUR HEART, THEN MUSIC WITH HER SILVER SOUND ...
WHY "SILVER SOUND"? WHAT'S YOUR ANSWER?

BECAUSE SILVER SOUNDS SWEET?
NO! WHAT ABOUT YOU?
UMM, I'D SAY "SILVER SOUND" BECAUSE MUSICIANS PLAY FOR SILVER?
NO! WHAT ABOUT YOU?
I DON'T KNOW.

THEN, I'LL TELL YOU. IT'S "MUSIC WITH HER SILVER SOUND" BECAUSE MUSICIANS HAVE NO GOLD.
THEN MUSIC WITH HER SILVER SOUND, BRINGS JOY AND PLEASURE RIGHT AROUND.

HE'S SO ANNOYING!
WHO CARES ABOUT HIM?
LET'S WAIT FOR THE **MOURNERS** TO COME BACK AND STAY FOR DINNER.

Act V, Scene I
THE OUTSKIRTS OF MANTUA – WEDNESDAY MORNING
I DREAMED THAT GOOD NEWS WAS ON ITS WAY. I HAVE A GOOD FEELING TODAY –
– I DREAMED THAT JULIET CAME AND FOUND ME DEAD. BUT THEN SHE GAVE ME THE KISS OF LIFE AND MADE ME FEEL LIKE A KING!
AH, SWEET LOVE CAN BRING JOY, EVEN IN DREAMS!
BALTHASAR!
DO YOU HAVE A LETTER FROM FRIAR LAURENCE?
HOW IS JULIET? HOW IS MY FATHER?
AGAIN, HOW IS JULIET?
NOTHING CAN BE WRONG IF SHE IS WELL.
I'M SORRY, SIR, BUT SHE'S DEAD.
HER BODY IS INSIDE THE CAPULET FAMILY TOMB. HER SOUL IS WITH THE ANGELS.
I SAW THEM BURYING HER IN THE TOMB MYSELF.

THAT CAN'T BE TRUE!!!
YOU KNOW WHERE I LIVE. BRING ME MY PEN AND PAPER AND SOME HORSES.
I'M LEAVING TONIGHT.
YOU SHOULDN'T RUSH, SIR. YOU JUST HEARD TERRIBLE NEWS.
JUST DO WHAT I TOLD YOU TO DO.
THWACK
DO YOU HAVE A LETTER FROM FRIAR LAURENCE?
NO, SIR.
IT DOESN'T MATTER. GET MOVING.
I'LL JOIN YOU SOON.
WELL, JULIET, I WILL REST WITH YOU TONIGHT AFTER ALL.
WHAT SHOULD I USE TO KILL MYSELF? I REMEMBER AN OLD AND POOR APOTHECARY WHO LIVES NEAR HERE.
HE MAKES POTIONS FROM HERBS.
HE IS VERY POOR –
– AND HIS SHOP IS FULL OF STRANGE THINGS.

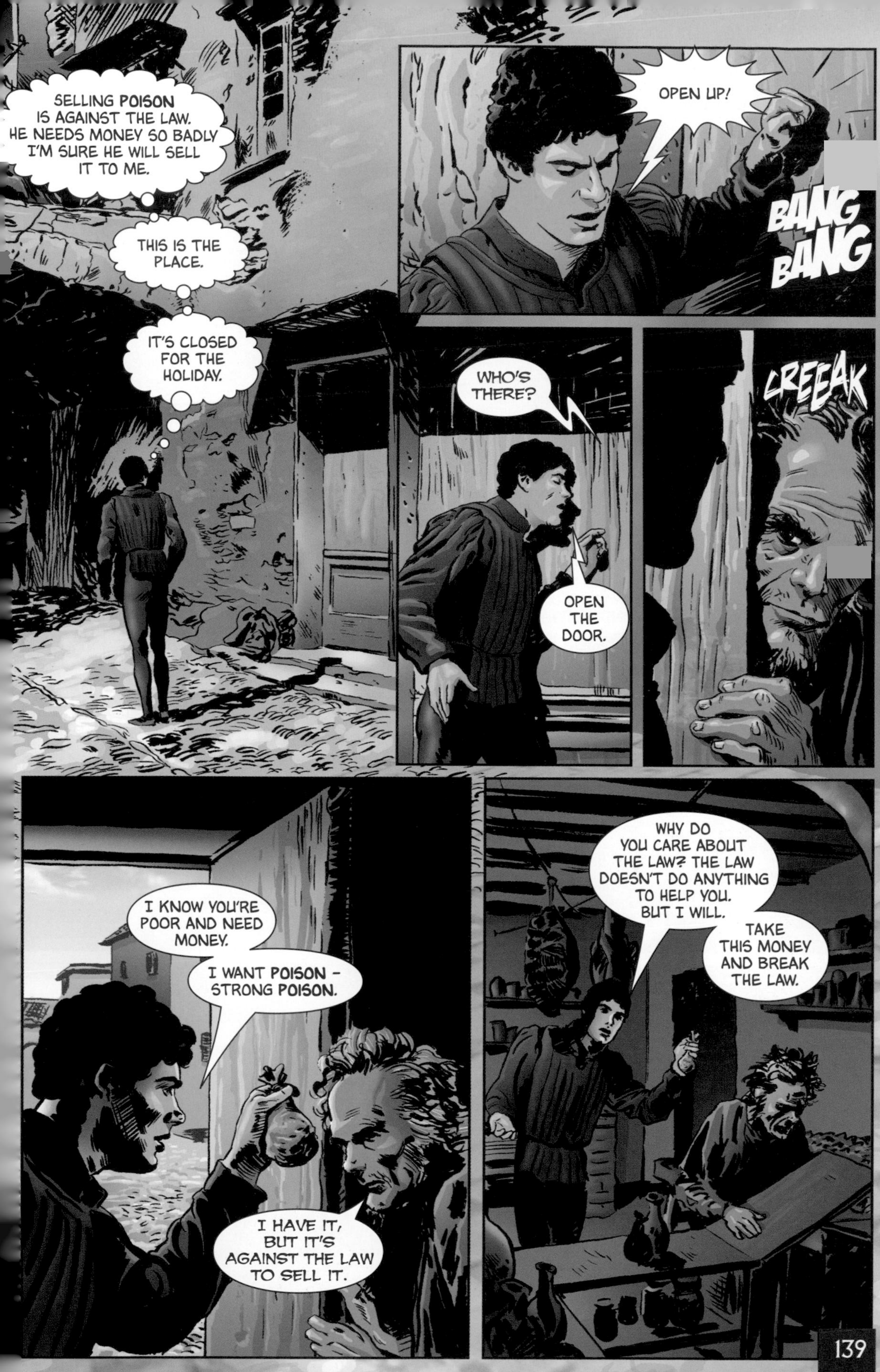

SELLING POISON IS AGAINST THE LAW. HE NEEDS MONEY SO BADLY I'M SURE HE WILL SELL IT TO ME.

THIS IS THE PLACE.

IT'S CLOSED FOR THE HOLIDAY.

OPEN UP!

BANG BANG

WHO'S THERE?

OPEN THE DOOR.

CREEEAK

ALL RIGHT, BUT IT DOESN'T MAKE THIS RIGHT.

GOOD MAN.

TAKE THIS. IT WILL KILL YOU **INSTANTLY**.

HERE'S YOUR MONEY –
CHINK KA-CHINK KA-CHINK CHINK
– AND THAT'S A WORSE **POISON** THAN ANYTHING YOU COULD SELL ME.

GOOD-BYE! BUY YOURSELF SOME FOOD AND PUT SOME MEAT ON YOUR BONES.
THE **POISON** YOU SOLD TO ME WILL TAKE ME TO JULIET!

Act V, Scene II
FRIAR LAURENCE'S CHURCH – WEDNESDAY EVENING
KNOCK KNOCK
FRIAR LAURENCE!
THAT SOUNDS LIKE FRIAR JOHN, BACK FROM MANTUA.

WHAT DID ROMEO SAY?
I WENT TO FIND ANOTHER FRIAR TO GO WITH ME. I MET UP WITH HIM AS HE WAS VISITING A HOUSE WITH SICK PEOPLE. BUT THE TOWN OFFICIALS THOUGHT WE MIGHT SPREAD THE SICKNESS, SO THEY LOCKED US IN THE HOUSE. I WASN'T ALLOWED TO LEAVE, SO I DIDN'T MAKE IT TO MANTUA.
WHO TOOK MY LETTER TO ROMEO?

NO ONE. I COULDN'T EVEN GET SOMEONE TO BRING IT BACK TO YOU.
OH, NO!

IT WAS IMPORTANT FOR ROMEO TO GET THIS LETTER.
THIS WILL CAUSE MANY, MANY PROBLEMS! FRIAR JOHN, GET ME A CROWBAR.
I WILL.

I'LL HAVE TO GO TO THE TOMB ALONE. JULIET WILL WAKE UP IN THREE HOURS.
SHE CAN STAY HERE WITH ME UNTIL I CAN GET ROMEO TO COME FOR HER.
THAT POOR LIVING CORPSE LOCKED UP INSIDE THAT TOMB!

Act V, Scene III
A CHURCHYARD CONTAINING THE CAPULET FAMILY TOMB – WEDNESDAY NIGHT
PUT OUT YOUR TORCH. THEN LIE DOWN BEHIND THOSE TREES AND LISTEN FOR ANYONE COMING THROUGH THE GRAVEYARD.
WHISTLE IF YOU HEAR ANYTHING.
CAPVLE
GIVE ME THOSE FLOWERS. NOW GO!
THIS GRAVEYARD SCARES ME!
HERE ARE FLOWERS FOR A BEAUTIFUL FLOWER. I'LL DO THIS EVERY NIGHT FROM NOW ON IN HONOR OF YOUR MEMORY.
SOMEONE'S COMING! WHAT TERRIBLE PERSON IS INTERRUPTING ME?
I'LL HIDE IN THE DARK.
GIVE ME THE TOOLS.
TAKE THIS LETTER AND DELIVER IT TO MY FATHER EARLY IN THE MORNING.

GIVE ME THE TORCH. I WANT YOU TO PRETEND THAT YOU DIDN'T SEE ME HERE.
I'M GOING INTO THE TOMB TO SEE MY WIFE'S FACE AND TO TAKE A RING FROM HER FINGER.
NOW GO AWAY. IF YOU COME BACK HERE TO CHECK ON ME, I'LL TEAR YOU TO PIECES.
I WON'T BOTHER YOU, SIR.
YOU'RE A GOOD FRIEND. TAKE THIS.
I HOPE YOU HAVE A LONG LIFE. GOOD-BYE.
I DON'T LIKE THIS. I'LL HIDE NEARBY AND WATCH.
INSIDE YOUR STOMACH YOU HAVE THE DEAREST CREATURE ON EARTH.
OPEN YOUR ROTTEN MOUTH!
RRRGGHHHH!
IT'S THAT MONTAGUE! THE ONE WHO MURDERED TYBALT AND MADE MY JULIET DIE OF A BROKEN HEART. WHAT'S HE DOING HERE?
I'LL ARREST HIM.

STOP WHAT YOU'RE DOING, MONTAGUE!
ARE YOU TRYING TO TAKE REVENGE ON THE DEAD?
COME WITH ME.
YOU ARE GOING TO DIE.
I CAME HERE TO DIE.
GO AWAY AND LEAVE ME ALONE.
LEAVE THIS PLACE! RUN AWAY!
?!?
DON'T MAKE ME COMMIT ANOTHER CRIME. I CAME HERE TO HARM MYSELF – NO ONE ELSE.
SAVE YOURSELF AND RUN AWAY!
CAPV
I'M NOT LISTING TO YOU. YOU'RE A LIAR!
I'M ARRESTING YOU BECAUSE YOU ARE A CRIMINAL!
IF YOU INSIST. HAVE IT YOUR WAY.

CLANG
CLANG
SSSSSWIIIIISH
AAAH!
THUMP
THEY'RE FIGHTING! I'LL CALL THE GUARD!
SWIIIISH

AAARGH!
SHNK
Oh! I'm going to die!
Please, lay me down next to Juliet in the **tomb**.
I WILL.
AAAAAARRGH
WAIT! IT'S COUNT PARIS, MERCUTIO'S RELATIVE. WHAT DID BALTHASAR SAY ON THE WAY HERE?
SOMETHING ABOUT COUNT PARIS MARRYING JULIET?
ZZZZZ
I SHOULD AT LEAST PUT HIM IN THE **TOMB**.

THIS ISN'T A GRAVE. IT'S MORE LIKE A LANTERN, FULL OF LIGHT FROM THE BEAUTIFUL JULIET.
BUT HOW CAN I CALL THIS "LIGHT"?
OH, MY LOVE! MY WIFE! YOU'RE STILL SO BEAUTIFUL.
IT'S LIKE YOU'RE STILL ALIVE.
TYBALT, IS THAT YOU?
FORGIVE ME FOR KILLING YOU. WE'LL BE EVEN SOON, WHEN I KILL MYSELF.
DEAR JULIET, WHY ARE YOU STILL SO BEAUTIFUL? DOES DEATH WANT YOU FOR HIMSELF?
HE CAN'T HAVE YOU. I'LL PROTECT YOU. I'LL NEVER LEAVE YOU AGAIN.
I'LL STAY HERE WITH THE WORMS AND END MY BAD LUCK.
ZZZZ

A LAST LOOK, A FINAL EMBRACE, AND A KISS TO END ALL KISSES. LET THIS POISON DO ITS WORK.
HERE'S TO MY LOVE!
WHAT A GOOD APOTHECARY! IT'S WORKING SO QUICKLY!
I'LL DIE WITH ONE LAST KISS.
I WISH I COULD RUN FASTER!
WHO'S THERE?
A FRIEND.
GOD BLESS YOU! TELL ME, GOOD FRIEND, WHAT IS THAT LIGHT COMING FROM THE CAPULET TOMB?
MY MASTER IS IN THERE.
CAPVLET
WHO IS IT?
ROMEO.
HOW LONG HAS HE BEEN THERE?
HALF AN HOUR.
COME WITH ME TO THE TOMB.
I CAN'T. HE SAID THAT HE'D KILL ME IF HE SAW ME BACK HERE.
I'LL GO ALONE, THEN. THIS DOESN'T LOOK GOOD.

WHEN I WAS SLEEPING OVER THERE, I DREAMED THAT ROMEO FOUGHT AND KILLED ANOTHER MAN.

ROMEO!

WHOSE BLOOD IS THIS?

AND WHY ARE THESE **WEAPONS** HERE IN THIS PEACEFUL PLACE?

ROMEO! HE'S SO **PALE**!

WHO ELSE?

COUNT PARIS, TOO!

HOW DID THIS HAPPEN?

JULIET'S WAKING UP.

DEAR **FRIAR** LAURENCE!

WHERE IS ROMEO?

WHAT'S THIS? A CUP?
POISON!
YOU DRANK IT ALL AND LEFT NONE FOR ME!
MAYBE THERE'S STILL SOME ON YOUR LIPS ...
YOUR LIPS ARE WARM.

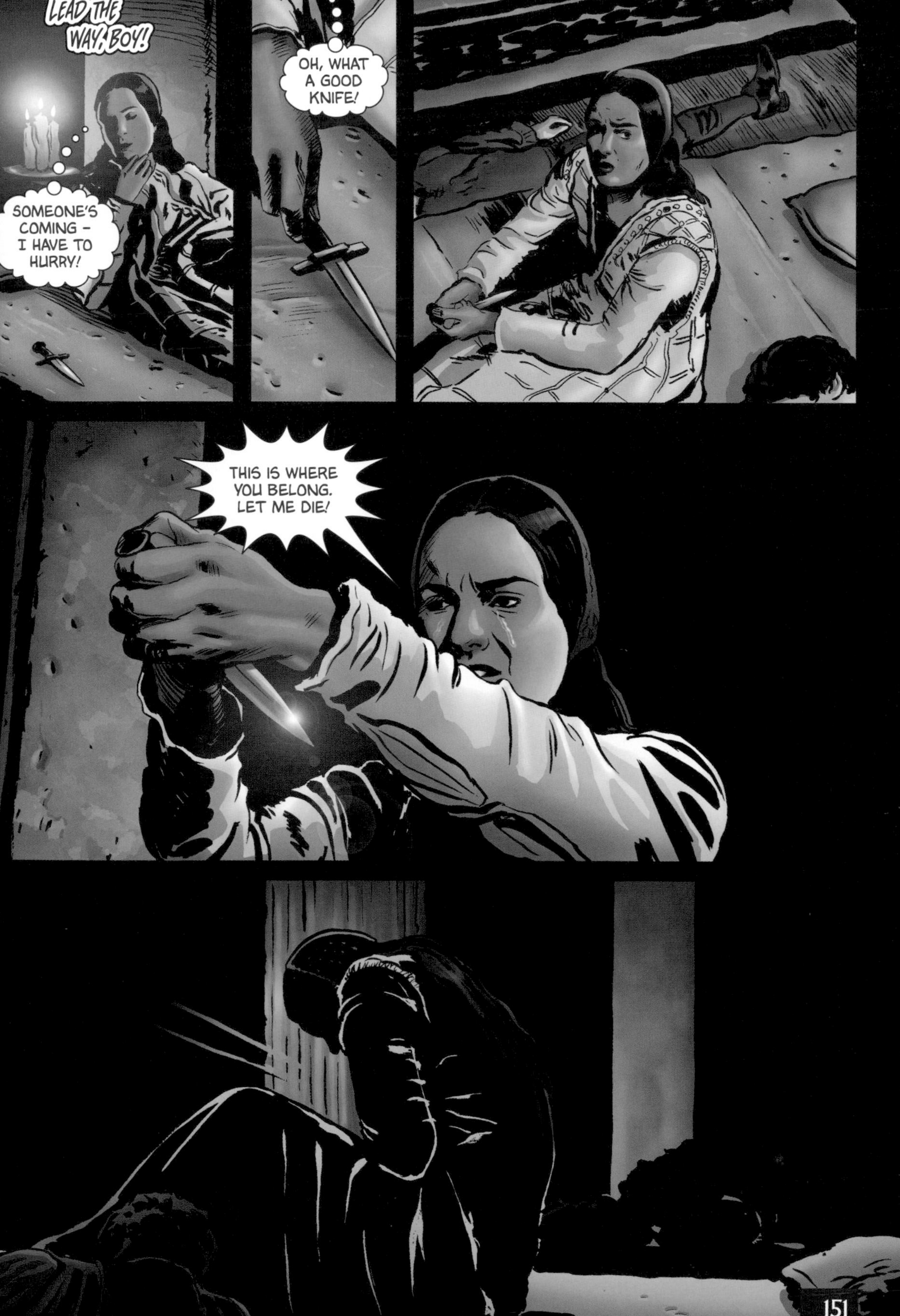
LEAD THE WAY, BOY!
SOMEONE'S COMING – I HAVE TO HURRY!
OH, WHAT A GOOD KNIFE!
THIS IS WHERE YOU BELONG. LET ME DIE!

THIS IS THE PLACE.
THE GROUND IS COVERED IN BLOOD. SEARCH THE **GRAVEYARD**! ARREST WHOEVER YOU FIND!

LOOK AT THIS!
COUNT PARIS HAS BEEN KILLED. AND JULIET IS WARM AND BLEEDING AS IF SHE HAS DIED A SECOND TIME.
GET THE PRINCE! GET THE CAPULETS AND MONTAGUES!
THE REST OF YOU, SEARCH THE AREA.
WE FOUND ROMEO'S **SERVANT** IN THE CHURCHYARD.
KEEP HIM HERE UNTIL THE PRINCE GETS HERE.
HERE'S A **FRIAR**. WE TOOK THESE TOOLS FROM HIM.
VERY **SUSPICIOUS**. HOLD THE **FRIAR**, TOO.
CAPVLET
WHAT HAPPENED?
WHAT'S ALL THE SCREAMING ABOUT?
THEY'RE SHOUTING "ROMEO," "JULIET," AND "COUNT PARIS!" AND THEY'RE RUNNING TOWARD THE **GRAVEYARD**.

WHY IS EVERYBODY SCREAMING AND CRYING?
COUNT PARIS HAS BEEN KILLED. ROMEO IS DEAD. AND JULIET, WHO WAS ALREADY DEAD, HAS BEEN KILLED AGAIN!
SEARCH THE AREA!
WE CAUGHT THIS **FRIAR** AND ROMEO'S **SERVANT** WITH TOOLS FOR OPENING **TOMBS**.
OH, MY!
OUR DAUGHTER IS BLEEDING! ROMEO'S KNIFE IS IN HER CHEST!
THIS IS A WARNING. IT IS A **SIGN** OF MY OWN DEATH.
COME HERE, LORD MONTAGUE, AND LOOK AT YOUR SON.
OH, NO! MY WIFE DIED TONIGHT. SENDING ROMEO AWAY BROKE HER HEART.
IS THERE ONLY MORE **MISERY**?

LOOK AND SEE.
IT'S NOT RIGHT FOR A SON TO DIE BEFORE HIS FATHER.
BE QUIET AND DON'T GET UPSET UNTIL WE CAN FIGURE OUT WHAT HAPPENED HERE.

IT WILL BE A WHILE BEFORE WE FIND OUT WHAT REALLY HAPPENED.

THE PIAZZA, VERONA – EARLY THURSDAY MORNING

BRING OUT THE **SUSPECTS.**

I AM THE ONE UNDER THE MOST **SUSPICION.**
I **BLAME** MYSELF, BUT I ALSO WANT TO EXPLAIN.

TELL US WHAT YOU KNOW.

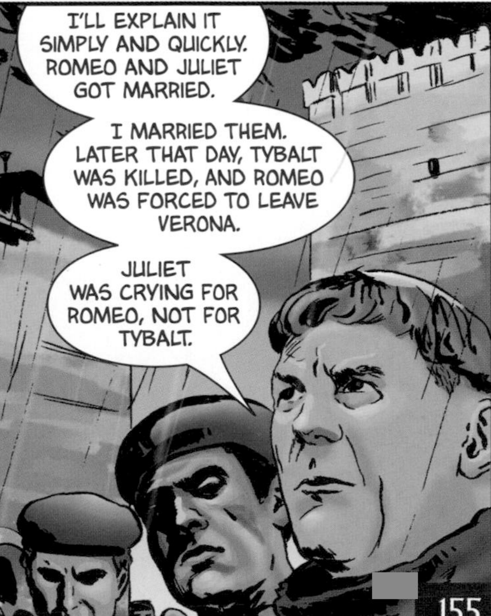

I'LL EXPLAIN IT SIMPLY AND QUICKLY. ROMEO AND JULIET GOT MARRIED.
I MARRIED THEM. LATER THAT DAY, TYBALT WAS KILLED, AND ROMEO WAS FORCED TO LEAVE VERONA.
JULIET WAS CRYING FOR ROMEO, NOT FOR TYBALT.

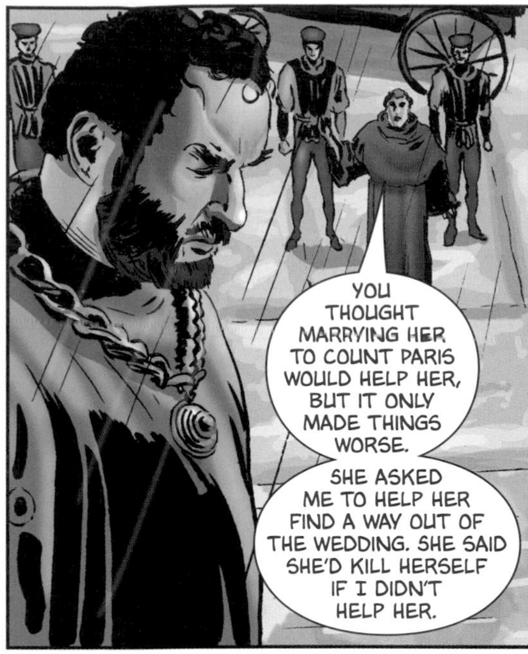
YOU THOUGHT MARRYING HER TO COUNT PARIS WOULD HELP HER, BUT IT ONLY MADE THINGS WORSE.
SHE ASKED ME TO HELP HER FIND A WAY OUT OF THE WEDDING. SHE SAID SHE'D KILL HERSELF IF I DIDN'T HELP HER.

I GAVE HER A SLEEPING **POTION** THAT MADE HER SEEM TO BE DEAD.
THE PLAN WAS FOR ROMEO TO COME BACK WHEN THE **POTION** WORE OFF. THEN THEY WOULD LIVE IN MANTUA UNTIL IT WAS SAFE FOR THEM TO RETURN TO VERONA.

I TOLD ROMEO ABOUT THE PLAN IN A LETTER THAT HE NEVER RECEIVED.
SO I WENT TO THE **TOMB** TO GET JULIET. I WAS GOING TO HIDE HER IN MY CHURCH UNTIL ROMEO CAME FOR HER.

WHEN I GOT THERE, I FOUND ROMEO AND COUNT PARIS ALREADY DEAD. JULIET WOKE UP, BUT SHE WOULDN'T LEAVE THE **TOMB** WITH ME.
I RAN AWAY BEFORE THE GUARDS ARRIVED. IT LOOKS LIKE SHE KILLED HERSELF.
THAT'S ALL I CAN TELL YOU. JULIET'S NURSE KNEW ABOUT THEIR MARRIAGE.

IF YOU THINK I AM TO **BLAME** FOR ANY OF THIS, **EXECUTE** ME.

YOU'RE AN HONEST AND HOLY MAN, FRIAR LAURENCE.
WHERE IS ROMEO'S SERVANT? DOES HE HAVE ANYTHING TO ADD?

I TOLD ROMEO ABOUT JULIET'S DEATH. WE CAME QUICKLY FROM MANTUA TO THIS GRAVEYARD.
ROMEO ASKED ME TO GIVE THIS LETTER TO HIS FATHER.

GIVE ME THE LETTER.
WHERE IS COUNT PARIS'S YOUNG SERVANT?

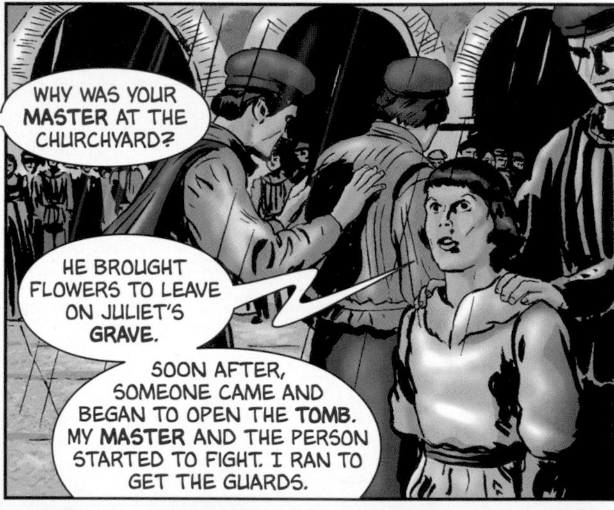
WHY WAS YOUR MASTER AT THE CHURCHYARD?
HE BROUGHT FLOWERS TO LEAVE ON JULIET'S GRAVE.
SOON AFTER, SOMEONE CAME AND BEGAN TO OPEN THE TOMB. MY MASTER AND THE PERSON STARTED TO FIGHT. I RAN TO GET THE GUARDS.

THIS LETTER PROVES THAT FRIAR LAURENCE'S STORY IS THE TRUTH.
ROMEO BOUGHT POISON AND USED IT TO KILL HIMSELF IN JULIET'S TOMB.

LORD CAPULET! LORD MONTAGUE!
DO YOU SEE THE DAMAGE YOUR HATRED FOR EACH OTHER HAS CAUSED?
BOTH YOUR CHILDREN HAVE BEEN KILLED. I HAVE ALSO LOST TWO MEMBERS OF MY FAMILY.
WE HAVE ALL BEEN PUNISHED!

GIVE ME YOUR HAND, LORD MONTAGUE. THIS IS YOUR WEDDING GIFT TO MY DAUGHTER. I'M NOT ASKING FOR ANYTHING ELSE.
BUT I WILL GIVE YOU MORE THAN THAT. I WILL MAKE A GOLD STATUE OF HER.
A STATUE OF HONEST AND FAITHFUL JULIET WILL BE SEEN IN VERONA FOREVER.
AND THERE WILL BE ONE OF ROMEO, STANDING BESIDE HER. THEY WILL REMIND PEOPLE OF THE SORROW CAUSED BY OUR FEUD.
AT LAST, THE FEUD WILL FINALLY END.
AND THOUGH THERE SHOULD BE GLADNESS,
OUR BROKEN HEARTS, TOO DIFFICULT TO MEND, ARE HEAVY IN THEIR SADNESS.
THERE NEVER WAS A STORY OF MORE WOE THAN THIS STORY OF JULIET AND HER ROMEO.
The End

Romeo and Juliet

Glossary

A

abbey /æbi/ – (abbeys) An abbey is a church with buildings attached to it in which monks or nuns live in or used to live in.
affect /əfɛkt/ – (affects, affecting, affected) If something affects a person or thing, it influences them or causes them to change in some way.
ancestor /ænsɛstər/ – (ancestors) Your ancestors are the people from whom you are descended.
apothecary /ə-'pä-thə-ker-ē/ – (apothecaries) An apothecary is someone who prepares and sells drugs or compounds for medicinal purposes.
appreciate /əpriʃieɪt/ – (appreciates, appreciating, appreciated) If you appreciate something, you like it because you recognize its good qualities; if you appreciate a situation or problem, you understand it and know what it involves.
ashamed /əʃeɪmd/ – If someone is ashamed, they feel embarrassed or guilty because of something they do or have done, or because of their appearance; if you are ashamed of someone or something, you feel embarrassed or guilty because of them.

B

banish /bænɪʃ/ – (banishes, banishing, banished, banishment) If someone or something is banished from a place or area of activity, they are sent away from it and prevented from entering.
bite one's thumb (at someone) /baɪt wʌnz θʌm (ət sʌmwʌn)/ – This is an action that shows hate for the person it is directed at.
blame /bləɪm/ – (blames, blaming, blamed) If you blame a person or thing for something bad, or if you blame something bad on somebody, you believe or say that they are responsible for it or that they caused it.
bless /blɛs/ – (blesses, blessing, blessed) When someone, such as a priest, blesses people or things, he or she asks for God's favor and protection for them.
bride /braɪd/ – (brides) A bride is a woman who is getting married or who has just gotten married.
bury /bɛri/ – (buries, burying, buried) To bury something means to put it into a hole in the ground and cover it up; to bury a dead person means to put their body into a grave and cover it with earth.

C

comfort /kʌmfərt/ – (comforts, comforting, comforted) Comfort is the state of being physically or mentally relaxed; comfort is a style of life in which you have enough money to have everything you need. If something offers comfort, it makes you feel less worried or unhappy.
concern /kənsɜrn/ – (concerns) Concern is worry about a situation; if a situation or problem is your concern, it is your duty or responsibility.
confession /kənfɛʃᵊn/ – (confessions) A confession is the telling of one's sins in order to receive forgiveness.
convince /kənvɪns/ – (convinces, convincing, convinced) If someone or something convinces you to do something, they persuade you to do it, if someone or something convinces you of something, they make you believe that it is true or that it exists.
corn /kɔrn/ – (corns) A corn is thickened skin on the top or side of a toe.
corpse /kɔrps/ – (corpses) A corpse is a dead body.
courtesy /kɜrtɪsi/ – Courtesy is politeness, respect, and consideration for others; a courtesy is something polite and respectful that you can say or do.
coward /kaʊərd/ – (cowards) A coward is someone who is easily frightened and avoids dangerous or difficult situations.
creature /kritʃər/ – (creatures) You can refer to any living thing that is not a plant as a creature.
crowbar /'krō-ber-ē/ – (crowbars) A crowbar is an iron or steel bar that is usually wedge-shaped at the working end for use as a pry or lever.
cruel /kruəl/ – Someone who is cruel deliberately causes pain or distress to people or animals.
crutch /krʌtʃ/ – (crutches) A crutch is a stick that someone with an injured foot or leg uses to support themselves when walking.
curse /kɜrs/ – (curses, cursing, cursed) If you curse, you use very impolite or offensive language, usually because you are angry about something; if you curse someone or something, you say impolite or insulting things about them because you are angry.
curtsey /'kərt-sē/ – (curtsies) To curtsey is an act of civility, respect, or reverence made mainly by women. It consists of a slight lowering of the body with bending of the knees.

D

damage /dæmɪdʒ/ – (damages) Damage is physical harm that is caused to an object.
dawn /dɔn/ – Dawn is the time of day when light first appears in the sky, just before the sun rises.
delay /dɪleɪ/ – (delays, delaying, delayed) If you delay doing something, you do not do it immediately or at the planned or expected time, but you leave it until later.
demand /dɪmænd/ – (demands, demanding, demanded) If you demand something, such as information or action, you ask for it in a very forceful way; if one thing demands another, the first needs the second in order to happen or be dealt with successfully.

E

embrace /ɪmbreis/ – (embraces, embracing, embraced) If you embrace someone, you put your arms around them in order to show affection for them.
enemy /ɛnəmi/ – (enemies) If someone is your enemy, they hate you or want to harm you.
evil /ivəl/ – (evils) Evil is used to refer to all the wicked and bad things that happen in the world; if you describe something or someone as evil, you mean that you think they are morally very bad and cause harm to people.
exchange /ɪkstʃeɪndʒ/ – (exchanges, exchanging, exchanged) If you exchange something, you replace it with a different thing, especially something that is better or more satisfactory.
execute /ɛksɪkyut/ – (executes, executing, executed) To execute someone means to kill them as a punishment.

F

faint /feɪnt/ – (faints, fainting, fainted) If you faint, you lose consciousness for a short time.
faithful /feɪθfəl/ – Someone who is faithful to a person, organization, or idea remains firm in their support for them.
feud /fyud/ – A feud is a quarrel in which two people or groups remain angry with each other for a long time.
formal /fɔrməl/ – Formal speech or behavior is very correct and serious, rather than relaxed and friendly, and is used especially in official situations.
fortune /fɔrtʃən/ – Fortune or good fortune is good luck; ill fortune is bad luck.
friar /'frī(-ə)r/ – (friars) A friar is a member of a Christian group who takes a vow of poverty and service to a community. Friars are supported by donations.
funeral /fyunərəl/ – (funerals) A funeral is a ceremony that is held when the body of someone who has died is buried or cremated.

G

gossip /gɒsɪp/ (gossips, gossiping, gossiped) If you gossip with someone, you talk informally, especially about other people or local events.
grave /greɪv/ – (graves) A grave is a place where a dead person is buried.
graveyard /greɪvyard/ – (graveyards) A graveyard is an area of land where dead people are buried.
grief /grif/ – Grief is a feeling of extreme sadness.
grieve /griv/ – (grieves, grieving, grieved) If you grieve over something, especially someone's death, you feel very sad about it.
groom /grum/ – (grooms) A groom is someone whose job is to look after the horses in a stable and keep them clean.

H

harm /harm/ – (harms, harming, harmed) To harm someone or something means to injure or damage them; harm is injury or damage to a person or thing.
heal /hil/ – (heals, healing, healed) When a broken bone or other injury heals, it becomes healthy and normal again; if you heal something, such as a disagreement, or if it heals, the situation is put right so that people are friendly or happy again.
heir /ɛər/ – (heirs) An heir is someone who has the right to inherit a person's money, property, or title when that person dies.
holy /hoʊli/ – Something that is holy is considered to be special because it is connected with God or a particular religion.
honor /ɒnər/ – Honor means doing what you believe to be right and being confident that you have done what is right; an honor is a special award that is given to someone, usually because they have done something good or because they are greatly respected.
honorable /ɒnərəbəl/ – If you describe people or actions as honorable, you mean that they are good and deserve to be respected and admired.

I

ignore /ɪgnɔr/ – (ignores, ignoring, ignored) If you ignore someone or something, you pay no attention to them.
inflict /ɪnflɪkt/ – To inflict harm or damage on someone or something means to make them suffer it.
insist /ɪnsɪst/ – (insists, insisting, insisted) If you insist that something should be done, you say so very firmly.
instantly /ɪnstəntli/ – Something that happens immediately is said to happen instantly.
insult /ɪnsʌlt/ – (insults, insulting, insulted) An insult is a rude remark or something a person says or does which insults you; if someone insults you, they say or do something that is rude or offensive.

J

jealous /dʒɛləs/ – If someone is jealous, they feel angry or bitter because they think that another person is trying to take away a lover or friend, or a possession, away from them.
justice /dʒʌstɪs/ – Justice is fairness in the way that people are treated; the justice of a cause, claim, or argument is its quality of being reasonable, fair, or right.

L

lame /leɪm/ – If you describe an excuse or argument as lame, you mean that it is poor or weak.
lantern /læntərn/ – (lanterns) A lantern is a lamp in a metal frame with glass sides.

lay to rest /leɪ tə rɛst/ – To lay to rest means to place a body in a grave or a tomb.
lecture /lɛktʃər/ – (lectures, lecturing, lectured) If someone lectures you about something, they criticize you or tell you how they think you should behave.
limp /lɪmp/ – If something is limp, it is soft or weak when it should be firm or strong.
lose (one's) temper /luz (wʌnz) tɛmpər/ – To lose one's tempers means to get angry very quickly and fly into a rage.

M

madam /mædəm/ – Madam is a very formal and polite way of addressing a woman.
mare /mɛər/ – (mares) A mare is an adult female horse.
mask /mæsk/ – (masks) A mask is something that you wear over your face for protection or to disguise yourself.
master /mæstər/ – (masters) A servant's master is the man that he or she works for.
mend /mɛnd/ – (mends, mending, mended) If you mend a tear or a hole in a piece of clothing, you repair it by sewing it.
mercy /mɜrsi/ – If someone in authority shows mercy, they choose not to harm or punish someone they have power over.
meteor /mitiər/ – (meteors) A meteor is a piece of rock or metal that burns very brightly when it enters Earth's atmosphere from space.
minstrel /'min(t)-strəl/ – (minstrels) A minstrel is a musical entertainer.
miserable /mɪzərəbᵊl/ – If you are miserable, you are very unhappy.
misery /mɪzəri/ – Misery is great unhappiness.
monster /mɒnstər/ – (monsters) A monster is a large, imaginary creature that looks very ugly and frightening.
mourner /mɔrnər/ – (mourners) A mourner is a person who attends a funeral.

N

nephew /nɛfyu/ – (nephews) Someone's nephew is the son of their sister or brother.
nightmare /naɪtmɛər/ – (nightmares) A nightmare is a very frightening dream.
nine lives /naɪn laɪvz/ – Cats are said to have nine lives because of their ability to survive falls from high places. It seems they return to life after fatal accidents.
noble /noʊbᵊl/ – If you say that someone is a noble person, you admire and respect them because they are unselfish and morally good; noble means belonging to a high social class and having a title.
nobleman /'nō-bəl-mən/ – (noblemen) A nobleman is a man of noble rank.
nonsense /nɒnsɛns/ – If you say that something spoken or written is nonsense, you think it is untrue or silly; you can use nonsense to refer to behavior that you think is foolish or that you disapprove of.

O

obsess /əbsɛs/ – (obsesses, obsessing, obsessed) If something obsesses you or if you obsess about something, you keep thinking about it and find it difficult to think about anything else.
orchard /ɔrtʃərd/ – (orchards) An orchard is an area of land on which fruit trees are grown.

P

pale /peɪl/ – Something that is pale is not strong or bright in color; if someone looks pale, their face looks a lighter color than usual, usually because they are ill, frightened, or shocked.
palm /pam/ – (palms) The palm of your hand is the inside part of your hand, between your fingers and your wrist.
passion /pæʃᵊn/ – Passion is a very strong feeling of love for someone; passion is a very strong feeling about something or a strong belief in something.
passionate /pæʃənɪt/ – A passionate person has very strong feelings about something or a strong belief in something.
picky /'pi-kē/ – A picky person is someone who is fussy or choosy.
pity /pɪti/ – If you say that it's a pity that something is true, you mean that you feel disappointment or regret about it.
play hard to get /hard tə gɛt/ – If someone plays hard to get, they pretend not to be interested or attracted by someone, usually to make the other person increase their efforts.
poison /plzən/ – (poisons) (n) Poison is a substance that harms or kills people or animals if they swallow or absorb it.
poison /plzən/ – (poisons, poisoning, poisoned) (v) To poison someone or something means to harm or damage them by giving them poison or putting poison into them.
potion /poʊʃᵊn/ – (potions) A potion is a drink that contains medicine, poison, or something that is supposed to have magical powers.
protest /prətɛst/ – (protests, protesting, protested) To protest means to say or show publicly that you object to something.

R

regards /rɪgɑrdz/ – Regards are greetings. You use regards as a way of expressing friendly feelings toward someone.
regret /rɪgrɛt/ – (regrets, regretting, regretted) If you regret something that you have done, you wish that you had not done it.

reveal /rɪvil/ – (reveals, revealing, revealed) To reveal something means to make people aware of it; if you reveal something that has been out of sight, you uncover it so that people can see it.
revenge /rɪvɛndʒ/ – Revenge involves hurting or punishing someone who has hurt or harmed you.
ruin /ruɪn/ – (ruins, ruining, ruined) To ruin something means to severely harm, damage, or spoil it; to ruin someone means to cause them to no longer have any money.

S

saint /seɪnt/ – (saints) A saint is someone who has died and been officially recognized and honored by the Christian church because his or her life was a perfect example of the ways Christians should live.
satisfy /sætɪsfaɪ/ – (satisfies, satisfying, satisfied) If someone or something satisfies you, they give you enough of what you want or need to make you pleased or contented; if you satisfy the requirements for something, you are good enough or have the right qualities to fulfill these requirements.
sensible /sɛnsɪbᵊl/ – Sensible actions or decisions are good because they are based on reasons rather than emotions.
sentence /sɛntəns/ – (sentences) In a law court, a sentence is the punishment that a person receives after they have been found guilty of a crime.
servant /sɜrvᵊnt/ – (servants) A servant is someone who is employed to work at another person's home, for example, as a cleaner or a gardener.
show off /ʃoʊ ɔf/ – (show offs) If you say that someone is a show off, you are criticizing them for trying to impress people by showing in a very obvious way what they can do or what they own.
sign /saɪn/ – (signs) If there is a sign of something, there is something that shows that it exists or is happening.
sorrow /sɒroʊ/ – (sorrows) Sorrow is a feeling of deep sadness or regret.
soul /soʊl/ – (souls) Your soul is the part of you that consists of your mind, character, thoughts, and feelings. Many people believe that your soul continues existing after your body is dead.
source /sɔrs/ – (sources) The source of something is the person, place, or thing which you get it from.
spirit /spɪrɪt/ – (spirits) Your spirit is the part of you that is not physical and that consists of your character and feelings.
spoke / spoʊk/ – (spokes) The spokes of a wheel are the bars that connect the outer ring to the center.
starve /stɑrv/ – (starves, starving, starved) If people starve, they suffer greatly from lack of food, which sometimes leads to their death; if a person is starved of something that they need, they are suffering because they are not getting enough of it.
stick-in-the-mud /stɪk ɪn ðə mʌd/ – If you call someone a stick-in-the-mud, you are saying that they lack enthusiasm or imagination.
stubborn /stʌbərn/ – Someone who is stubborn or who behaves in a stubborn way is determined to do what they want and is very unwilling to change their mind.
suffocate /sʌfəkeɪt/ – (suffocates, suffocating, suffocated) If someone suffocates, they die because there is no air for them to breathe.
surrounded /səraʊnd/ – If a person or thing is surrounded by something, that thing is situated all around them.
suspect /sʌspɛkt/ – (suspects) A suspect is a person who the police or authorities think may be guilty of a crime.
suspicion / səspɪʃᵊn/ – (suspicions) Suspicion is the belief or feeling that someone has committed a crime or done something wrong; a suspicion is a feeling that something is probably true or is likely to happen.
suspicious /səspɪʃəs/ – If you are suspicious of someone or something, you do not trust them.
swear / swɛər/ – (swears, swearing, swore) If you swear to do something, you promise in a serious way that you will do it.

T

take (someone) down a peg or two /teɪk (sʌmwʌn) daʊn ə pɛg ər tu/ – To take someone down a peg or two is to lower someone's high opinion of themselves.
tomb /tum/ – (tombs) A tomb is a stone structure containing the body of a dead person.
torch /tɔrtʃ/ – (torches) A torch is a long stick or device with a flame at one end, used to provide light, to set things on fire, or to melt or cut something.

V

villain /vɪlən/ – (villians) A villain is someone who deliberately harms other people or breaks the law in order to get what he or she wants.

W

weapon /wɛpən/ – (weapons) A weapon is an object, such as a gun, a knife, or a missile, which is used to kill or hurt people in a fight or war.
well /wɛl/ – (wells) A well is a hole in the ground from which a supply of water is extracted.
whistle /wɪsᵊl/ – (whistles, whistling, whistled) When you whistle, you make sounds by forcing your breath out between your lips or teeth.
wimp /wɪmp/ – (wimps) If you call someone a wimp, you disapprove of them because they lack confidence or determination, or because they are often afraid of things.
wisdom /wɪzdəm/ – Wisdom is the ability to use your experience and knowledge in order to make sensible decisions or judgments.
woe /woʊ/ – Woe is great sadness.

William Shakespeare

(c. 1564–1616 AD)

Many people believe that William Shakespeare was the world's greatest writer in the English language.

The actual date of Shakespeare's birth is unknown. Most people accept that he was born on April 23, 1564. Records tell us that he died on the same date in 1616 at the age of 52.

Shakespeare grew up in Stratford-upon-Avon, a small English village. He was the oldest son of John Shakespeare and Mary Arden, and the third of eight children. The Shakespeares were a well-respected family. John Shakespeare, a tradesman who made gloves and traded leather, became the mayor of the town a few years after Shakespeare was born.

Shakespeare was lucky to survive childhood. Sixteenth-century England was filled with diseases, such as smallpox, tuberculosis, typhus, and dysentery. Most people did not live more than 35 years. Three of Shakespeare's seven siblings died from what was probably the bubonic plague, a contagious disease that was very common at the time.

As a child, Shakespeare went to the local schools where he learned to read and write. Eventually, he also studied Latin and English literature. In 1582, when Shakespeare was 18, he married Anne Hathaway. Hathaway, who was eight years older than Shakespeare, was the daughter of a local farmer. They had three children: Susanna, born on May 26, 1583, and twins, Hamnet and Judith, born on February 2, 1585. Hamnet died from the bubonic plague in 1596.

In 1587, Shakespeare moved to London to be an actor and playwright. His wife and children stayed in Stratford-upon-Avon. Although Shakespeare performed in many plays, it was his playwriting that got the most attention. He soon became famous throughout England. When Queen Elizabeth I died in 1603, her cousin James became king. Shakespeare's acting company often performed for James I. In return, the king allowed Shakespeare's acting company to be called The King's Men.

Shakespeare wrote 38 plays, 154 sonnets, and many poems between 1590 and 1613. No one has ever found any of Shakespeare's original scripts. This makes it difficult to know exactly when each play was written. It was common for plays to change constantly as they were performed. Shakespeare wrote the script and then made changes with each performance. The plays we know today come from written copies taken from different stages of each play. Because of this, there are different versions of many of Shakespeare's plays.

In 1599, Shakespeare's acting company built the Globe Theatre, one of the largest theaters in England. Thousands of people crammed into the theater for each performance. In 1613, the theater burned down. Although the theater was rebuilt in 1614, Shakespeare stopped writing and left London. He returned to Stratford-upon-Avon to live with his family. He died just three years later.

The cause of Shakespeare's death is not known. He was buried at the Church of the Holy Trinity In Stratford-upon-Avon. The words written on his gravestone are believed to have been written by Shakespeare himself:

Good friend for Jesus' sake forbear
To dig the dust enclosed here!
Blessed be the man that spares these stones,
And cursed be he that moves my bones.

In his will, Shakespeare left most of his possessions to his oldest daughter, Susanna. The only thing he left to his wife was his "second best bed." Nobody knows what this gift meant. Shakespeare's last direct descendant, a granddaughter named Elizabeth, died in 1670.

The History of Romeo and Juliet

Romeo and Juliet is one of Shakespeare's most famous plays. Because of this, many people assume that Shakespeare created the story of *Romeo and Juliet* himself. However, like most of Shakespeare's plays, *Romeo and Juliet* is adapted from a story that already existed. (*The Tempest* is Shakespeare's only play without a known source.)

The first version of *Romeo and Juliet* appeared in a story by Masuccio Salernitano around 1460. In this story, Mariotto Mignanelli and Gianozza Saraceni of Siena fall in love and are secretly married by a friar. Soon after this, Mariotto fights with and kills an important citizen of the town. Mariotto is banished from the town, and Gianozza's father forces her to marry someone else. The friar creates a potion for Gianozza that makes her seem to be dead. Mariotto hears about her death before the friar can bring Gianozza to him. Mariotto returns to Siena, where he is captured and executed. Gianozza goes to live in a convent and soon dies from grief. Salernitano claimed that the characters and events of this story were based on a true story.

Salernitano's story became the inspiration for Luigi da Porto's *Giulietta e Romeo* in 1530. Da Porto set his version of the story in Verona. Da Porto was inspired by two castles just outside the city of Verona. One was owned by the Capuleti family, and the other was owned by the Montecchi family. Da Porto's version introduced the idea of the feuding families. This story has an even more tragic ending than the one in Shakespeare's play. In da Porto's version, Romeo kills himself beside Giulietta, who he believes is dead. However, as he is dying, he sees Giulietta wake up. When Giulietta sees Romeo dead, she stabs herself with Romeo's knife. Like Salernitano, Da Porto also claimed that his story was based on real events.

In 1554, an Italian writer named Matteo Bandello published his own version of the story, which he also called *Giulietta e Romeo*. This story was much more popular than the versions that came before it. It was translated into English and became the inspiration for a 3,020-line poem by Arthur Brooke called *The Tragicall Historye of Romeus and Juliet*. Brooke's poem, which was written in 1562, has all the main characters found in Shakespeare's play, although with some spelling differences: Romeus Montagew, Juliet Capilet, Prince Escalus, Tybalt, Paris, Friar Lawrence, and Juliet's nurse.

Although Shakespeare added his own ideas to the story, all of the events of his play are found in Brooke's poem. It is possible that Shakespeare worked with other sources, too. He may have read the French translation of Bandello's novel as well as an English version of the story by William Painter called *Palace of Pleasure*. However, it is Brooke's poem that is most similar to Shakespeare's play. The greatest difference between the two versions is that, while the events in Brooke's poem take place over nine months, Shakespeare reduced the time to just five days.

Shakespeare's *Romeo and Juliet* was written before the Globe Theatre was built, while Elizabeth I was the Queen. It was the first tragedy that Shakespeare wrote. He finished it early in his career, probably in 1594 or 1595. It was first printed in 1597.

Even though Shakespeare's plays were extremely popular, only a few records exist of actual performances. The earliest official recording of a production of *Romeo and Juliet* doesn't occur until as late as 1662.

Until the 1660s, it was illegal for women and girls to perform on stage. Until this time, all the parts in *Romeo and Juliet*, including Juliet, were played by men.

Romeo and Juliet was popular with audiences from its earliest performances. However, there have been periods when the play was performed with some major changes. For example, in the seventeenth century, some productions had Romeo and Juliet not only survive, but live long, happy lives together.

By the nineteenth century, *Romeo and Juliet* had become one of Shakespeare's most famous and most frequently performed plays. It is performed all over the world and has been adapted countless times. There have been dozens of operas and ballets based on the story of *Romeo and Juliet* and more than eighteen film versions. There have also been modern stories and plays that are based on *Romeo and Juliet*. The most famous example is the stage musical *West Side Story*, in which two rival street gangs take the place of the Montagues and the Capulets, and the characters of Tony and Maria take the place of Romeo and Juliet.

Although *Romeo and Juliet* was written over 400 years ago, it remains as popular with readers and audiences today as it was back in Shakespeare's day.

Important Quotations

Location	Shakepeare's Original	Adapted Text
Act II, Scene II Page 55	"But, soft! What light through yonder window breaks? It is the east and Juliet is the sun."	"But, wait! What is the light shining through that window? It is the east, and Juliet is the sun!"
Act II, Scene II Page 55	"See, how she leans her cheek upon her hand! O that I were a glove upon that hand, that I might touch that cheek!"	"She looks so beautiful, leaning her cheek on her hand. I wish I was a glove on that hand, so that I could touch her cheek."
Act II, Scene II Page 56	"O Romeo, Romeo! wherefore art thou Romeo? Deny thy father, and refuse thy name."	"Oh, Romeo, Romeo! Why do you have to be a Montague? Forget your father and change your name."
Act II, Scene II Page 56	"What's in a name? That which we call a rose by any other name would smell as sweet."	"Names aren't important. The flower that we call a rose would smell just as sweet even if it was called something else."
Act II, Scene II Page 58	"O, swear not by the moon, the fickle moon, the inconstant moon, that monthly changes in her circle orb, Lest that thy love prove likewise variable."	"Oh, don't swear on the moon. It changes every month. I don't want your love to change the way the moon does."
Act II, Scene II Page 62	"Goodnight, goodnight! Parting is such sweet sorrow that I shall say goodnight till it be morrow."	"Good night again. Leaving each other is sweet but filled with sorrow. I will say goodnight to you until it is tomorrow!"
Act V, Scene III Page 148	"O true apothecary! Thy drugs are quick. Thus with a kiss I die."	"What a good apothecary! It's working so quickly!"
Act V, Scene III Page 150	"Poison? Drunk all, and left no friendly drop to help me after?"	"Poison! You drank it all and left none for me!"

OTHER CLASSICAL COMICS TITLES:

Henry V 1-4240-2877-9

Frankenstein 1-4240-3184-2

Great Expectations 1-4240-2882-5

Macbeth 1-4240-2873-6

Jane Eyre 1-4240-2887-6

COMING SOON:

The Tempest 1-4240-4296-8